Buttercream
Basics

Buttercream Basics

Learn the Art of Buttercream Decorating

Carey Madden

Author of *Sensational Buttercream Decorating*

Robert **ROSE**

For complete cataloguing information, see page 256.

Disclaimer

The recipes in this book have been carefully tested by our kitchen and our tasters. To the best of our knowledge, they are safe and nutritious for ordinary use and users. For those people with food or other allergies, or who have special food requirements or health issues, please read the suggested contents of each recipe carefully and determine whether or not they may create a problem for you. All recipes are used at the risk of the consumer.

We cannot be responsible for any hazards, loss or damage that may occur as a result of any recipe use.

For those with special needs, allergies, requirements or health problems, in the event of any doubt, please contact your medical adviser prior to the use of any recipe.

Design and Production: Daniella Zanchetta/PageWave Graphics Inc.

Editor: Sue Sumeraj

Proofreader: Kelly Jones

Indexer: Gillian Watts

Photographer: Daniel Jackson

Cover image: French Kiss (pages 154–157)

Additional images: p.7 White & grey pattern©iStockphoto.com/Yulla_Lesovaya; p.10 Icing chocolate cake with spatula©iStockphoto.com/violleta; p.11 Blue triangle chevron pattern ©iStockphoto.com/the_corner; p.21 Pom pom chrysanthemum pattern©iStockphoto.com/ Nocturnus; p.25 Yellow cake©iStockphoto.com/cobraphoto; p.35 Pink diamond pattern ©iStockphoto.com/Kannaa; p.57 Teal diamond pattern©iStockphoto.com/Oksancia; p.95 Purple semicircle pattern©iStockphoto.com/FrankRamspott; p.105 Orange geometric pattern©iStockphoto.com/helga_wigandt; p.185 Damask wallpaper pattern©iStockphoto.com/ fatmayilmaz; p.221 Pink dots pattern©iStockphoto.com/Oksancia.

Published by Robert Rose Inc.

120 Eglinton Avenue East, Suite 800, Toronto, Ontario, Canada M4P 1E2

Tel: (416) 322-6552 Fax: (416) 322-6936

www.robertrose.ca

Printed and bound in Canada

1 2 3 4 5 6 7 8 9 TCP 25 24 23 22 21 20 19 18 17

··

To my most dear friends — you know who you are.
Thank you for being the icing on the cake,
the cherry on top and the primary ingredient
for an altogether sweet life.

·································

♥

Contents

Introduction

I've come to think that some form of creative expression is necessary for a fully realized life. I use the term "creative expression" loosely to include tinkering with car engines, building model airplanes, crocheting, creating bottle cap art or playing an instrument — anything that elevates us above the banality of everyday life. Creative acts are proof positive of our best and most unique selves. They are the greatest gifts to those around us and to ourselves for their ability to stop time, allowing us to be both intensely present and somewhere else altogether better.

Buttercream Basics will walk you through every step of transforming raw ingredients into a fully formed and decorated piece of edible art. But cake is more than the combined ingredients or even the finished product. Every new endeavor includes the possibility of triumph or disappointment, sunken cakes or singular bites of bliss, cakes that evoke pride or those you'd rather feed to the dog. Cake is a manifestation of your individual creativity, a statement of affection and practical fare that nourishes the body and soul in a way that only butter and sugar whipped by hand and with heart can do. No matter the result, the benefit will be greater than the cake served.

I've included in this book my own confectionary triumphs and setbacks, and everything I could think of that I've picked up along the way that could possibly lead you toward decorating success. We are all makers, tinkerers, craftspeople and artists. Bake, decorate and eat with abandonment. Let loose the creative noose of perfection, high expectations, self-criticism and judgement. You are the very best part of your cake.

Acknowledgments

Tremendous thanks and gratitude to cake decorator extraordinaire and creative crackerjack Leigh Polous, whose assistance made the cakes beautiful and the book better, and whose support and friendship made it all a hell of a good time. Her tenacity and courage in creating art and a life worthy of her talent continues to be an example to me.

Much appreciation to publisher Bob Dees for his insight and acumen, and to all the staff at Robert Rose for their parts in making this project possible.

I feel great appreciation for and indebtedness to editor Sue Sumeraj, whose experience, analytical ability, sharp eye and wisdom crafted my disordered thoughts into a logical and ordered book. Sue, you complete me!

Photographer Daniel Jackson's enthusiasm, fine art aesthetic and indefatigable quest for random props made the cakes — and, by extension, me — look good, and his affable personality brought joy and sanity to the set. Thank you, Dan and Don Bethman, for your dedication.

Many thanks to all the folks at PageWave Graphics, and especially designer Daniella Zanchetta for her enthusiasm in tackling a complex project, her organizational abilities and her supreme good taste. Thanks also to proofreader Kelly Jones for her discerning reading and keen observations.

A warm and grateful nod to Sophie Cook, Cara Anselmo, Miina Matsuoka, Alan Littlewood, Candace Toth, Angelina Blandino, Margie McBirnie Morrison, Christina Madden, Jamie Madden and Alma Madden for their generous insights and opinions; to my faithful friends and benefactors Jill Sloane, Jeffrey Elliot and Matthew Weinberg; and to Daniel Westiner and Other Animal Coffee Roasters for sharing space and demonstrating massive tolerance and good cheer in the face of total buttercream takeover.

Continued love and gratitude to my mother and brother.

How to Use This Book

Taking time to explore the first three chapters of this book will increase your familiarity with the tools and techniques necessary for baking cakes, making icing and decorating. Once you're acquainted with this fundamental information, you can jump into the projects anywhere you choose. Information or skills needed from other chapters or projects are noted in each project for easy cross-referencing.

Project Features

- **Bits & Nibbles:** These hints and tips will help make decorating easy and fast.

- **Piece of Cake:** Simplifications of the projects to make them even easier.

- **Up Your Game:** Intermediate to advanced techniques for even cooler effects.

- **Phraseology:** Explanations of new, important or obscure terminology.

- **Cake Debate:** Answers to frequently asked questions about common or interesting decorating issues.

- **Learn from My Mistakes:** Frank revelations of what I could have done differently and advice on how to avoid potential pitfalls.

Bits & Nibbles

- When starting a project or recipe, read it through in its entirety *before* beginning. The information in the Bits & Nibbles boxes and elsewhere can be essential to the project execution.

- The terms "icing" and "buttercream" are used interchangeably and refer to the same delicious edible substance.

- Keep cakes and presentation surfaces secure on a spinning turntable by placing a thin, damp kitchen towel or paper towel underneath.

- Practice decorating using plain, uncolored buttercream so you don't waste food coloring on initial blunders. The practice icing can be scraped off and reused.

- For clearer photographs of the step-by-step instructions in this book, the cakes are, in most cases, pictured directly on the turntable throughout the decorating process. However, if the project directions tell you to center the cake on the presentation surface before beginning to decorate, you should make sure to do so, as it will be much more difficult to transfer the cake once it is fully decorated.

Chapter 1

Tools You Can't Live Without

Like most pursuits, cake decoration involves tools that are specific to the medium, and when inspiration strikes, having the right tools best supports the expression of that inspiration.

Tool Guide

The list below lays out the tools you will find handy when preparing the projects in this book. You won't necessarily need to have every tool on this list on hand: certain tools, such as cookie cutters, a cake leveler or a fancy cake stand, are nice to have but are not essential items for decorating. And many of these are very common kitchen tools that you likely already own, so you'll just need to supplement with any extra items called for in the equipment list for the cake you wish to make.

The most essential tools are described in more detail in the Decorating Survival Kit, below.

- Stand mixer
- Mixing bowls in various sizes
- Baking pans
- Parchment paper
- Wire cooling racks
- Double boiler
- Candy thermometer
- Turntable
- Serrated knife
- Cake leveler
- Toothpicks or skewers
- Cardboard rounds
- Pastry bags
- Kitchen scissors
- Couplers
- Decorating tips
- Food coloring
- Storage containers
- Mason jars or drinking glasses
- Apron
- Paper towels
- Kitchen towels
- Large offset spatula
- Small offset spatula
- Straight spatula
- Rubber spatula
- Various combs
- Flexible plastic card
- Cake plates, cake stands or anything else you choose to use as a presentation surface
- Squeeze bottle of corn syrup
- Water spritzer
- Various cookie cutters
- Candy molds and templates
- Rose nail
- Small scissors
- Ribbon
- Tweezers
- Various sprinkles
- Pencil
- Paintbrush

Decorating Survival Kit

There are certain tools that are either absolutely necessary for decorating or so handy as to justify keeping them close at hand. Here is a list of the items that make up the Decorating Survival Kit.

Turntable

A well-built turntable is an investment piece that will last you a lifetime. Avoid turntables that wobble when rotated. Keep your turntable clean and well-greased with food-grade high-quality oil.

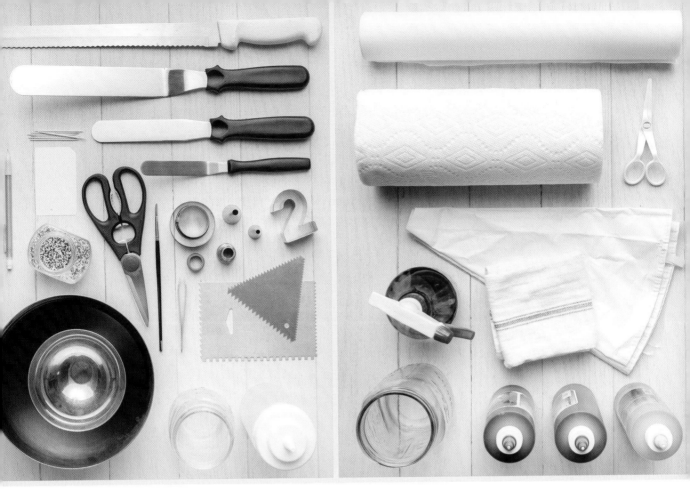

Serrated Knife

A good long, sturdy knife, with a blade 8 to 12 inches (20 to 30 cm) in length, is essential for crowning and torting cakes (see page 36 for instructions on crowning and torting). Keep your cake knife sharp and separate from others, using it exclusively for delicate cake work.

Cardboard Rounds

Not a tool traditionally found in home kitchens, cardboard rounds become invaluable when torting cakes into multiple layers and transferring iced cakes from turntable to refrigerator or presentation surface. Cardboard rounds cost pennies and offer tremendous support and protection for your treasured work of edible art. Keep a handful of rounds in various common sizes on hand.

Metal Spatulas

Metal spatulas are as vital to the cake decorator as paintbrushes are to the artist. Keep in your tool kit a large offset spatula, a small offset spatula and a large straight spatula. Reserve these spatulas for decorating exclusively. Any nicks to the spatulas' finish can cause lines and indents when you use them to ice a cake.

Rubber Spatulas

Rubber spatulas are indispensable for mixing colors and scraping buttercream icing from bowls, so keep a stash of them handy.

Bowls and Storage Containers

The fun of mixing multiple colors requires many bowls and containers, and it's a downer to have to halt progress to scrub a bowl. A storage container can often be used for both mixing and storing. The dollar store is a great place to stock up on these items.

Food Coloring

At a minimum, keep on hand a supply of the primary and secondary colors, plus black; that way, you'll have the ability to mix any color. See page 44 for details on food coloring and mixing colors.

Squeeze Bottle of Corn Syrup

Corn syrup is called "baker's glue" because it is both edible and adhesive. Cakes are attached to the presentation surface with corn syrup, and some projects in the book also find other uses for the sticky stuff. You can make your own squeeze bottle of corn syrup, but some brands already come with a flip lid and a small pouring spout.

Rectangular Comb

A large rectangular comb with a serrated edge and a straight edge is essential for icing cakes that are smooth and have right angles (see Polished, page 59, for instructions on icing a cake smooth).

Pastry Bags

Because they are easier to grip and they don't add more plastic to landfills, my preference is to pipe with reusable fabric bags, but in a pinch I will use disposable plastic bags. If you choose to work with reusable pastry bags, buy bags with fabric that is thin and easy to gather in one hand and won't allow oil to seep through. This usually means investing in high-quality bags. Fabric bags will last many years if cared for properly. Cleaning them properly includes turning them inside out, removing the couplers, washing them with soapy boiling water and allowing them to dry *completely* before storing them. If all this sounds like too much work, there is the option of disposable plastic bags, which are convenient and require no upkeep.

As for size, a large bag can be filled with small quantities of buttercream, but a small bag can fit only so much, leading to messy overflows and requiring frequent refills. I suggest 14- or 16-inch (35 or 40 cm) bags, which are fairly large but still easy to manipulate.

Decorating Tips

Once you're familiar with the multitude of decorating tips (see pages 16–19) available, you'll start to establish favorites. You might prefer a certain size round tip for inscribing cakes, a specific star tip for borders and a particular brand for making roses.

Though not necessarily expensive, decorating tips become valuable for how they support your artistic expression. Take good care of your tips, keeping them clean and dry, and free of grease and rust. Be gentle with your tips: they can easily be crushed underfoot or can become dented and misshapen if thrown in the bottom of a sink, underneath a pile of dishes. Keep tips far away from the gaping maw of the garbage disposal!

Rose Nail

A rose nail is a small, round stainless steel disk attached to a thin nail-like shaft, and is essential for making ribbon roses (see page 213). I like to keep two rose nails on hand, because if one gets lost or damaged, there's no other tool that can act as a substitute.

Small Scissors

Scissors are a handy tool for all sorts of reasons, but they are critical for transferring ribbon roses from the rose nail to the cake.

Kitchen Towel and Paper Towels

Decorating with grease-laden buttercream and drippy food coloring can be a messy business. Having a damp kitchen towel and a roll of paper towels always within arm's reach makes for a cleaner and happier decorating experience. Choose kitchen towels that are particularly absorbent and use them exclusively for decorating, because certain food colorings stain.

Decorating Tip Guide

The decorating tip is the instrument that allows you to manipulate buttercream icing into wildly expressive and beautiful cake decorations. Tips are essentially small metal cones with openings cut in various shapes, creating distinctive decorations when buttercream icing is pushed through. Tips come in a huge array of sizes and shapes, and are easily identified by a number stamped into their surface.

There are two basic sizes of tips: smaller standard-size tips, which can be used alone or paired with a coupler, and large tips, which are used without a coupler. (See Preparing the Pastry Bag on page 42 for further information on couplers.)

This tip guide (pages 16–19) includes all the tips that are used to make the projects in this book (plus a few more that you might find useful), and these tips are a great start to creating your own tip collection. You may want to purchase multiples of favorite tips to avoid washings between bag and color changes.

Cleaning Tips

You can quickly clean a tip by holding it under fast-running hot water. When you're finished with a decorating project, all of the tips you used should be thoroughly washed and sanitized. Boil the tips, couplers and coupler rings in an appropriately sized saucepan — and boil them twice. During the first boil, the majority of the buttercream is released; during the second boil, add dish soap to remove all traces of grease. Use a fine-mesh sieve to drain the tips between boils. Rest clean tips on a baking sheet lined with paper towels or a kitchen towel until they are completely dry, making sure to separate tips that have nested together during the cleaning process.

Rose Tips

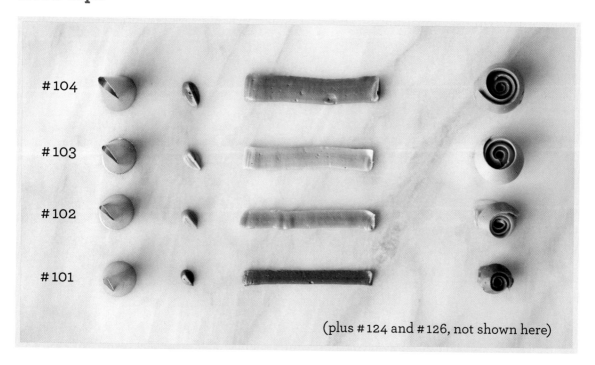

#104

#103

#102

#101

(plus #124 and #126, not shown here)

Large Round Tips

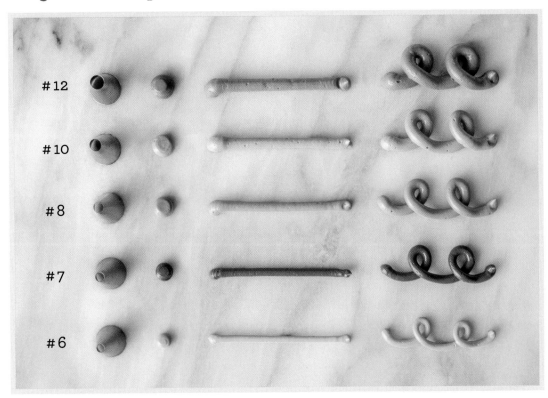

#12
#10
#8
#7
#6

Small Round Tips

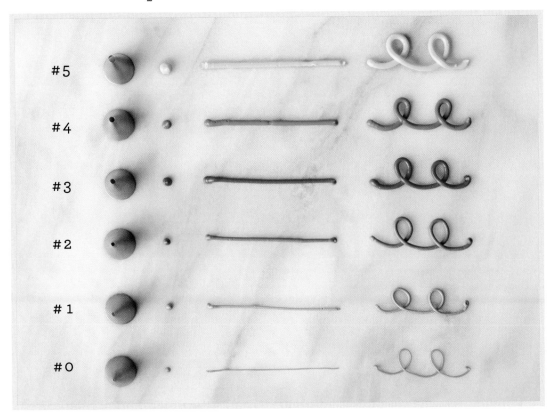

#5
#4
#3
#2
#1
#0

Open Star Tips

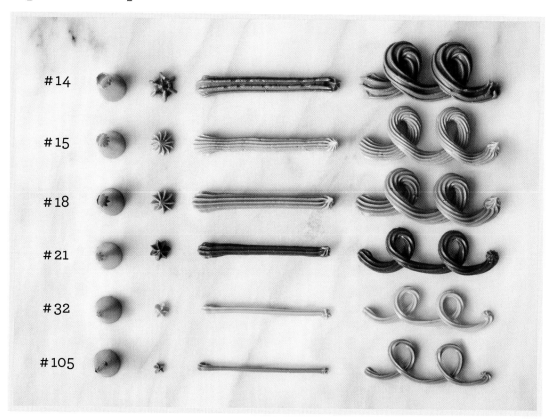

#14

#15

#18

#21

#32

#105

Closed Star Tips

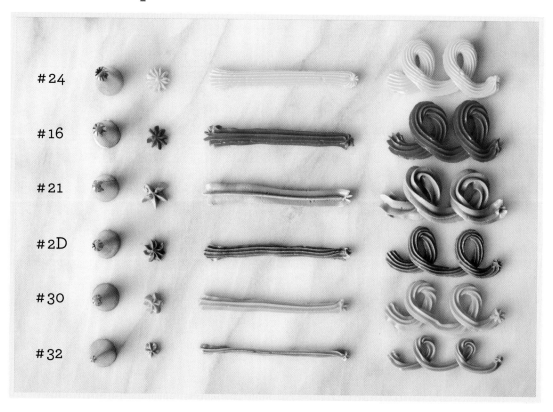

#24

#16

#21

#2D

#30

#32

Miscellaneous Tips

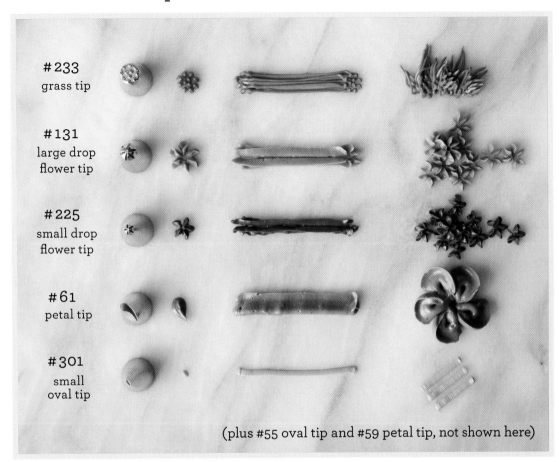

#233
grass tip

#131
large drop
flower tip

#225
small drop
flower tip

#61
petal tip

#301
small
oval tip

(plus #55 oval tip and #59 petal tip, not shown here)

Leaf Tips

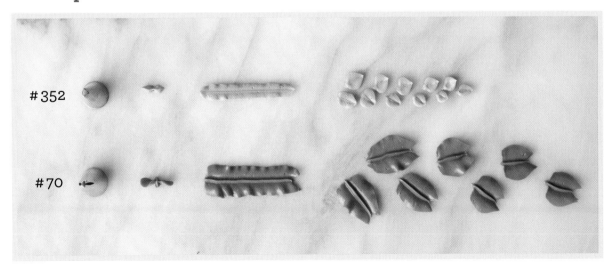

#352

#70

Chapter 2
Cake and Icing Recipes

Like judging the cover of a book, a cake cannot be judged by its decoration alone. The original function of a cake is as food, and the decoration… well, that's just the icing on top. Let form follow function and bake a cake that is worthy of your decorating prowess. The two cake recipes in this chapter will showcase your decoration to best effect.

As for the icing, for those who have never had a taste of Swiss meringue buttercream, it can be a revelation — silky-smooth and decadently rich without being heavy. It's a wonder that an icing with so much buttery goodness can also be as light as a cloud.

Yellow Butter Cake

Makes 2 cake layers

With a good yellow cake, it's possible to taste the individual ingredients that go into making it — butter, sugar, eggs, vanilla and buttermilk — and at the same time, the ingredients combine to form something altogether new and better. Enjoy these most humble ingredients in their most regal form.

Variations

For four 4-inch (10 cm) cake layers: Prepare the batter for the 6-inch (15 cm) cake layers and divide it equally among four prepared 4-inch (10 cm) round cake pans. Bake for about 25 minutes, then let cool as directed. If not using all four cake layers immediately, double-wrap them with plastic wrap and store them in the freezer for later use.

For 24 cupcakes or 48 mini cupcakes: Line 24 cups of muffin pans or 48 cups of mini muffin pans with paper liners. Prepare the batter for the 6-inch (15 cm) cake layers and divide it equally among prepared muffin cups. Bake in upper and lower thirds of oven, for equal heat distribution, for about 18 minutes. For even baking, switch pans between racks and turn them halfway through. Let cool as directed.

- Preheat oven to 325°F (160°C)
- Stand mixer, fitted with paddle attachment (see Bits & Nibbles, page 24)
- Two 6-inch (15 cm), 8-inch (20 cm) or 10-inch (25 cm) round cake pans, sprayed with nonstick cooking spray, bottoms lined with parchment paper

For 6-inch (15 cm) cake layers

1½ cups	all-purpose flour	375 mL
3 tbsp	potato starch	45 mL
1 tsp	baking powder	5 mL
¾ tsp	baking soda	3 mL
½ tsp	salt	2 mL
1 cup	buttermilk	250 mL
1½ tsp	vanilla extract	7 mL
1 cup	granulated sugar	250 mL
½ cup	unsalted butter, softened	125 mL
2	large eggs	2
1	large egg yolk	1

For 8-inch (20 cm) cake layers

2¾ cups	all-purpose flour	675 mL
⅓ cup	potato starch	75 mL
2 tsp	baking powder	10 mL
1 tsp	baking soda	5 mL
1 tsp	salt	5 mL
2 cups	buttermilk	500 mL
1 tbsp	vanilla extract	15 mL
2 cups	granulated sugar	500 mL
1 cup	unsalted butter, softened	250 mL
3	large eggs	3
2	large egg yolks	2

Variations

For a double-layer sheet cake: Prepare the batter for the 8-inch (20 cm) cake layers to make each 1- to 1¼-inch (2.5 to 3 cm) layer. You will need to mix up two batches of the batter to make two thin layers that can be filled and stacked. Do not try to mix two batches at once, as it's unlikely your mixing bowl is large enough to handle the double load. Pour each batch of batter into a 15- by 11-inch (38 by 28 cm) sheet cake pan (see Bits & Nibbles) and bake for about 35 minutes, then let cool as directed.

For a single-layer sheet cake: Prepare the batter for the 10-inch (25 cm) cake layers to make one thicker sheet cake that can be iced and served on its own. Pour the batter into a 15- by 11-inch (38 by 28 cm) sheet cake pan (see Bits & Nibbles) and bake for about 45 minutes, then let cool as directed.

For 10-inch (25 cm) cake layers

4 cups	all-purpose flour	1 L
½ cup	potato starch	125 mL
1 tbsp	baking powder	15 mL
1½ tsp	baking soda	7 mL
1½ tsp	salt	7 mL
3 cups	buttermilk	750 mL
1½ tbsp	vanilla extract	22 mL
3 cups	granulated sugar	750 mL
1½ cups	unsalted butter, softened	375 mL
5	large eggs	5
3	large egg yolks	3

1. Using a fine-mesh sieve, sift together flour, potato starch, baking powder, baking soda and salt into a medium bowl.

2. In a measuring cup or small bowl, combine buttermilk and vanilla. Set aside.

3. In stand mixer bowl, cream sugar and butter on low speed until well blended, light and fluffy. Beat in eggs, one at a time, beating well after each addition, then beat in yolk(s) until well blended.

4. With the mixer on low speed, alternately beat in flour mixture and buttermilk mixture, making three additions of flour and two of buttermilk, and beating just until well blended.

5. Using a rubber spatula, briefly stir the batter to ensure that all the ingredients are incorporated, then divide the batter equally between prepared cake pans, leveling the tops with the spatula.

6. Bake in preheated oven for about 35 minutes for 6-inch (15 cm) cakes, 40 minutes for 8-inch (20 cm) cakes or 45 minutes for 10-inch (25 cm) cakes, or until a tester inserted in the center comes out clean.

7. Let cool in pans on wire racks for 10 minutes, then remove from pans and let cool completely on racks before slicing and filling.

Bits & Nibbles

- If you don't have a stand mixer, you can use a heavy-duty handheld mixer to make this cake. Use the mixer and a large bowl for step 3, then use a silicone spatula or wooden spoon to incorporate the flour and buttermilk mixtures by hand as directed in step 4.

- Parchment rounds can be purchased precut in multiple sizes from bakery supply stores and online, but you can just as easily cut your own by tracing the bottom of the baking pan with a pen or pencil and using scissors to cut the circle ¼ inch (5 mm) smaller than the outline.

- When separating the yolks for this cake, be sure to save the egg whites for making buttercream icing.

- The addition of potato starch to the flour reduces the overall protein content, allowing enough gluten for structure but not so much that the cake becomes tough and chewy. The result is a cake that is tender and moist, with a fine, even crumb. Potato starch can be found at some grocery stores, most health food stores and online. It should not be confused with potato flour, which is a completely different product.

- Oven temperatures vary and can affect cooking time. Avoid opening the oven before 15 minutes have passed, but start checking for doneness 10 minutes before the allotted time. A cake is done when a toothpick, skewer or knife is inserted and comes out clean or with just a few crumbs attached. You can also tell when a cake is finished by gently poking the center. A cake that is thoroughly baked will not jiggle; it will be cushiony and the finger indentation will spring back and disappear.

- If making one of the sheet cakes described in the variations, you want to use a 15- by 11-inch (38 by 28 cm) pan. For home bakers, this is considered a sheet pan, but if you're comparing it to a cake that you might get from a commercial bakery, it would seem closer to a half sheet cake. Keep in mind that a full commercial-size sheet cake might not fit into your oven or fridge, and the extra-large size makes working with one unwieldy.

Triple Chocolate Cake

Semisweet chocolate, cocoa powder and mini chocolate chips pack this cake with enough chocolate punch to satisfy even the most ardent chocolate admirer. The sour cream contributes a smooth denseness without being heavy, and the addition of both butter and vegetable oil makes for a flavor-rich cake that is particularly moist.

Variation

For four 4-inch (10 cm) cake layers: Prepare the batter for the 6-inch (15 cm) cake layers and divide it equally among four prepared 4-inch (10 cm) cake pans. Bake for about 25 minutes, then let cool as directed. If not using all four cake layers immediately, double-wrap them with plastic wrap and store in the freezer for later use.

- Preheat oven to 350°F (180°C) for 6- or 8-inch (15 or 20 cm) cakes or to 325°F (160°C) for 10-inch (25 cm) cakes
- Stand mixer, fitted with paddle attachment (see Bits & Nibbles, page 29)
- Two 6-inch (15 cm), 8-inch (20 cm) or 10-inch (25 cm) round cake pans, sprayed with nonstick cooking spray, bottoms lined with parchment paper

For 6-inch (15 cm) cake layers

1 cup	all-purpose flour	250 mL
⅓ cup	unsweetened cocoa powder	75 mL
1 tsp	baking soda	5 mL
½ tsp	salt	2 mL
½ cup	boiling water	125 mL
1½ oz	semisweet chocolate, coarsely chopped	45 g
1 tsp	instant coffee granules	5 mL
½ cup	sour cream	125 mL
1 tbsp	vegetable oil	15 mL
1½ tsp	vanilla extract	7 mL
½ tsp	white vinegar	2 mL
1 cup	packed brown sugar	250 mL
¼ cup	unsalted butter, softened	60 mL
1	large egg	1
1	large egg yolk	1
½ cup	mini chocolate chips, tossed with 1 tbsp (15 mL) flour	125 mL

For 8-inch (20 cm) cake layers

2 cups	all-purpose flour	500 mL
⅔ cup	unsweetened cocoa powder	150 mL
2 tsp	baking soda	10 mL
1 tsp	salt	5 mL
1 cup	boiling water	250 mL
3 oz	semisweet chocolate, coarsely chopped	90 g
2 tsp	instant coffee granules	10 mL
1 cup	sour cream	250 mL
2 tbsp	vegetable oil	30 mL
1 tbsp	vanilla extract	15 mL

Variations

For 24 cupcakes or 48 mini cupcakes: Line 24 cups of muffin pans or 48 cups of mini muffin pans with paper liners. Prepare the batter for the 6-inch (15 cm) cake layers and divide it equally among prepared muffin cups. Bake in upper and lower thirds of oven, for equal heat distribution, for about 18 minutes. For even baking, switch pans between racks and turn them halfway through. Let cool as directed.

For a double-layer sheet cake: Prepare the batter for the 8-inch (20 cm) cake to make each 1- to 1¼-inch (2.5 to 3 cm) layer. You will need to mix up two batches of the batter to make two thin layers that can be filled and stacked. Do not try to mix two batches at once, as it's unlikely your mixing bowl is large enough to handle the double load. Pour each batch of batter into a 15- by 11-inch (38 by 28 cm) sheet cake pan (see Bits & Nibbles) and bake at 325°F (160°C) for about 35 minutes.

1 tsp	white vinegar	5 mL
2 cups	packed brown sugar	500 mL
½ cup	unsalted butter, softened	125 mL
2	large eggs	2
2	large egg yolks	2
1 cup	mini chocolate chips, tossed with 2 tbsp (30 mL) flour	250 mL

For 10-inch (25 cm) cake layers

3 cups	all-purpose flour	750 mL
1 cup	unsweetened cocoa powder	250 mL
1 tbsp	baking soda	15 mL
1½ tsp	salt	7 mL
1½ cups	boiling water	375 mL
4½ oz	semisweet chocolate, coarsely chopped	140 g
1 tbsp	instant coffee granules	15 mL
1½ cups	sour cream	375 mL
3 tbsp	vegetable oil	45 mL
1½ tbsp	vanilla extract	22 mL
1½ tsp	white vinegar	7 mL
3 cups	packed brown sugar	750 mL
¾ cup	unsalted butter, softened	175 mL
3	large eggs	3
3	large egg yolks	3
1½ cups	mini chocolate chips, tossed with 3 tbsp (45 mL) flour	375 mL

1. Using a fine-mesh sieve, sift together flour, cocoa, baking soda and salt into a medium bowl.

2. Pour boiling water into another medium bowl. Stir in chopped semisweet chocolate and coffee granules until completely melted and dissolved. Let cool slightly. Whisk in sour cream, oil, vanilla and vinegar. Set aside.

3. In stand mixer bowl, cream brown sugar and butter on low speed until well blended, light and fluffy. Beat in egg(s), one at a time, beating well after each addition, then beat in yolk(s) until well blended.

Variation

For a single-layer sheet cake:
Prepare the batter for the 10-inch (25 cm) cake layers to make one thicker sheet cake that can be iced and served on its own. Pour the batter into a 15- by 11-inch (38 by 28 cm) sheet cake pan (see Bits & Nibbles) and bake at 325°F (160°C) for about 45 minutes, then let cool as directed.

4. With the mixer on low speed, alternately beat in flour mixture and chocolate mixture, making three additions of flour and two of chocolate and beating just until well blended.

5. Using a rubber spatula, briefly stir the batter to ensure that all the ingredients are incorporated. Gently fold in chocolate chips. Divide the batter equally between prepared cake pans, leveling the tops with the spatula.

6. Bake in preheated oven for about 35 minutes for 6-inch (15 cm) cakes, 40 minutes for 8-inch (20 cm) cakes or 45 minutes for 10-inch (25 cm) cakes, or until a tester inserted in the center comes out clean.

7. Let cool in pans on wire racks for 10 minutes, then remove from pans and let cool completely on racks before slicing and filling.

Bits & Nibbles

- If you don't have a stand mixer, you can use a heavy-duty handheld mixer to make this cake. Use the mixer and a large bowl for step 3, then use a silicone spatula or wooden spoon to incorporate the flour and chocolate mixtures by hand as directed in step 4.

- You can replace the boiling water and coffee granules with piping-hot strongly brewed coffee or espresso, using an equal amount to the boiling water.

- When separating the yolks for this cake, be sure to save the egg whites for making buttercream icing.

- The purpose of tossing the chocolate chips with flour is to make them a little more "sticky" and buoyant, so that they don't all sink to the bottom of the cake.

- Use leftover butter wrappers in place of parchment paper to line your baking pans. Trim them to the correct shape with scissors. I keep my extras stacked neatly in a sealable baggie in the fridge.

- Oven temperatures vary and can affect cooking time. Avoid opening the oven before 15 minutes have passed, but start checking for doneness 10 minutes before the allotted time. A cake is done when a toothpick, skewer or knife is inserted and comes out clean or with just a few crumbs attached. You can also tell when a cake is finished by gently poking the center. A cake that is thoroughly baked will not jiggle; it will be cushiony and the finger indentation will spring back and disappear.

- If making one of the sheet cakes described in the variations, you want to use a 15- by 11-inch (38 by 28 cm) pan. For home bakers, this is considered a sheet pan, but if you're comparing it to a cake that you might get from a commercial bakery, it would seem closer to a half sheet cake. Keep in mind that a full commercial-size sheet cake might not fit into your oven or fridge, and the extra-large size makes working with one unwieldy.

Swiss Buttercream Icing

Makes about 5 cups (1.25 L)

The most extraordinary characteristic of Swiss meringue buttercream icing is its subtle sweetness. Many icings rely on sugar for structure and stiffness, to a gritty and sweetly cloying effect. Swiss-style icing primarily uses egg whites for structure, which frees the sugar to act principally as a sweetener.

Swiss buttercream has other extraordinary qualities: it has the ability to stretch and bend and has a pliable firmness that allows for the creation of multidimensional decorations.

Variation

The Swiss meringue buttercream recipe featured here has a neutral vanilla flavor that pairs nicely with any cake flavor. The flavor can easily be altered with the addition of a fragrant oil, extract, jam, curd, purée, melted and cooled chocolate or nut butter. Add flavoring in small quantities until you have achieved the desired taste. Added flavorings may change the consistency and texture of the icing, so reserve plain vanilla-flavored buttercream for decorating.

- Double boiler (see Bits & Nibbles, opposite)
- Stand mixer, fitted with whisk attachment (see Bits & Nibbles, opposite)
- Candy thermometer

1½ cups	granulated sugar	375 mL
Pinch	salt	Pinch
1 cup	large egg whites (about 8)	250 mL
½ tsp	cream of tartar	2 mL
2 tsp	vanilla extract	10 mL
2 cups	unsalted butter, softened (1 lb/454 g)	500 mL

1. In the top of a double boiler, over gently simmering water, whisk together sugar, salt and egg whites. Heat, whisking constantly, until sugar is dissolved and the mixture reaches 140°F (60°C).

2. Pour egg mixture into stand mixer bowl and add cream of tartar and vanilla. Beat on medium speed until firm peaks form and the meringue is cooled to room temperature.

3. If necessary, cut block of butter lengthwise into 4 sticks. Using a small offset spatula, cut butter into small pats, about ⅓ inch (8 mm) in size. Add butter to the cooled meringue, one pat at a time, beating on medium speed until all of the butter is incorporated and the icing is smooth and satiny.

American Buttercream Icing

The easygoing, laid-back cousin to Swiss buttercream, American-style buttercream requires no heating, cooling or finicky whipped egg whites, making it a fast and easy alternative to Swiss buttercream. American buttercream is beloved and is a nostalgic favorite for many, but it is stiffer, denser and sweeter than Swiss. The decorations in this book are created using Swiss meringue buttercream exclusively. American buttercream can be substituted, but you'll need to allow for an adjustment period to become familiar with the different consistency and texture.

Bits & Nibbles

- If you don't have a double boiler, fill a medium saucepan with 1 inch (2.5 cm) of water and place a deep, heatproof bowl on top, making sure the bowl does not touch the water (it is the steam that will gently heat the eggs).

- If you don't have a stand mixer, you can use a heavy-duty handheld mixer to make the buttercream. It will take quite a long time and can get tiring to hold the mixer, so a kitchen helper to takes turns with would be very handy.

- Neglecting the consistent whisking of delicate egg whites, or a burner that is too hot, can transform the gentle pasteurization process into a cooking process, resulting in bobbing bits of scrambled eggs. Egg solids can easily be removed by running the pasteurized meringue base through a fine-mesh sieve into the mixing bowl. Use a rubber spatula to press as much of the liquid through the mesh as possible.

- Even a minute trace of grease can inhibit eggs from fully inflating into meringue. Before beginning this recipe, use a paper towel dampened with lemon juice or vinegar to wipe clean all equipment that will come in contact with the egg whites, including the mixer bowl, the whisk and a rubber spatula.

- Whipping egg whites to firm peaks can take anywhere from 10 to 25 minutes. Beating on medium speed will allow time for the egg white mixture to cool and will keep your mixer from overheating.

- Egg whites can form firm peaks before reaching room temperature. Do not add the butter to the whipped meringue until it has cooled completely. To determine whether the meringue has cooled sufficiently, hold your hand against the outside of the bowl to gauge the general temperature.

- Softened butter should still be slightly cool and pliable, not glossy with oil and on the verge of imminent collapse. If your kitchen tends toward hot, leave the butter out for a shorter duration or place it briefly in the fridge to firm up before adding it to the whipped egg whites.

continued next page…

Bits & Nibbles

- Butter is added to the whipped meringue in small portions. You can cut the butter into neat squares and then add it square by square into the mixing bowl, or you can save yourself a step by slicing each pat of butter directly into the bowl, one at a time, after the meringue has cooled to room temperature.

- This recipe can be doubled if your stand mixer is large enough: it needs to have a 5-quart (5 L) capacity. If you're working with a handheld mixer, it's best to make multiple single batches.

- Because the eggs have been pasteurized, buttercream can be stored at room temperature for a few days or in the fridge for 2 weeks, and it freezes beautifully. Make life easier by whipping up multiple batches of buttercream in advance of decorating.

Cake Debate

Q: Dear Carey, Help! I whipped the egg whites to glossy perfection and the whole kit and caboodle deflated and curdled into a sloshy mess once I started adding the butter. I'm completely freaked out, and I think my buttercream is done for. Can it be saved?

Please help, One Deflated Egg Short of a Full Carton

A: Dear ODESOAFC, Please do not despair. As frightening as it is to watch carefully pasteurized meringue and edible gold bricks (butter) turn into cottage cheese, all is not lost. This is a common occurrence experienced by professionals and novices alike. I'm no food scientist, but my best guess is that the cause has something to do with the temperature of the butter and the temperature of the whipped egg whites. Rein in the panic as best you can and just keep beating, then beat some more. Keep the faith: your buttercream will more than likely miraculously right itself.

Phraseology

Pasteurize: When making Swiss buttercream, it's necessary to pasteurize the egg whites. To pasteurize a food means to expose it to an elevated temperature for a period of time sufficient to destroy certain microorganisms without radically altering taste or quality.

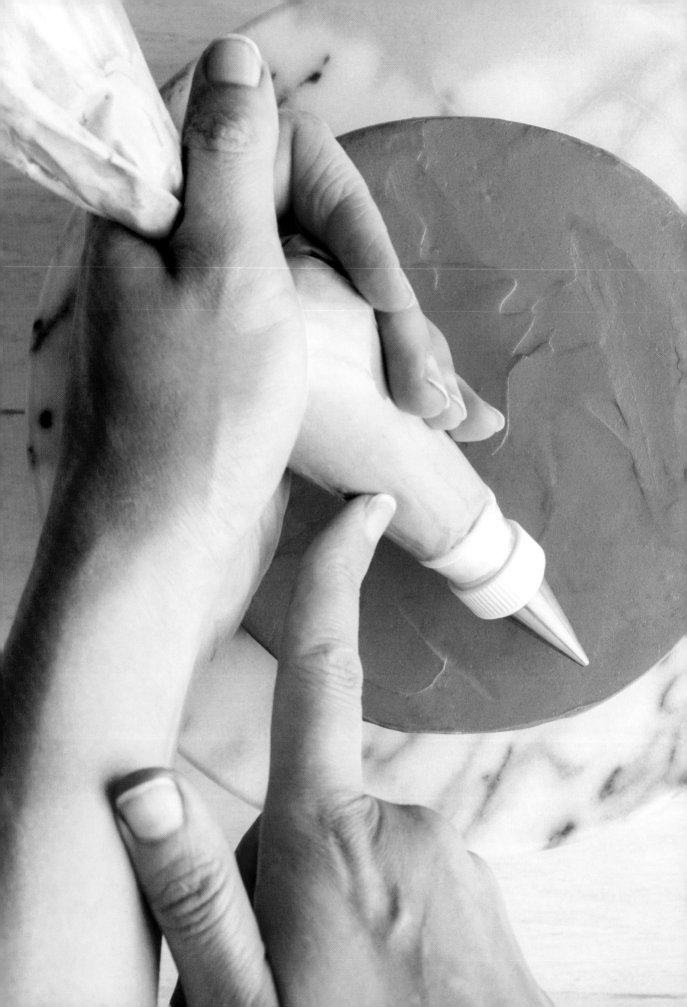

Chapter 3

Getting Started

You're armed with a cake decorating survival kit, your Swiss buttercream is a vision of satiny perfection, and your cake could be used as a memory foam pillow. Bridle your enthusiasm just long enough to read this chapter and create a foundation of basic skills and knowledge that will bolster the odds for cake decorating success.

Preparing the Cake
Crowning and Torting

An easy tell that a cake is homemade is the pleasing dome on top. I love a handcrafted cake, but there are times when a flat, level surface is advantageous, especially when you're adding decoration. Slicing a dome off the top of a cake is called crowning. Slicing a cake into multiple horizontal layers, usually to add a filling, is called torting. For consistent, even layers, it is important to use a turntable so that you can easily rotate the cake while slicing.

To keep the cake in place, cup your nondominant hand against the side of the cake. Holding the knife horizontal, place the blade against the cake on the opposite side.

Applying downward pressure with your nondominant hand, spin the turntable slowly, allowing the blade to make a shallow cut all the way around the cake.

Using the first shallow cut as your guide, continue spinning the turntable as you apply gentle pressure to the knife, allowing it to slice farther into the cake.

Keeping the knife horizontal, continue applying pressure to the knife and spinning the turntable until the knife slices completely through the cake, removing the dome or cutting the cake into layers.

Alternative Method

1

Insert toothpicks all the way around the side of the cake, using your knife, spatula or ruler as a vertical guide, depending on where you need to make the cut.

2

Holding the knife horizontal, place the blade just above the toothpicks and carefully slice across the cake, exerting gentle pressure while spinning the turntable.

Bits & Nibbles

- Make sure to peel parchment paper from the bottom of the cake before slicing it.

- Cakes are best cut using a serrated knife that is 8 to 12 inches (20 to 30 cm) in length. The blade should be longer than the diameter of the cake.

- A great way to ensure that your cake layers are level and even is to anchor your elbow against the side of your waist while slicing. Allow your forearm to move back and forth at the same point along your waist while slicing, but never up and down.

- Don't feel like you need to add serious elbow grease to the business of slicing. Let the knife and the turntable do all the work. Allow for multiple rotations of the turntable to cut a single layer. If your knife is sharp enough, you won't even have to saw back and forth, just apply light pressure and spin.

- When you're torting a cake, the thin layers can be fragile and can easily break apart when they are moved, especially with larger cakes. After slicing through the cake, carefully slide a cardboard round the same size as the cake beneath the layer for easy transport.

- If you find wielding a large knife terrifying, there are tools you can purchase that make crowning and torting a cake less intimidating. Look for cake levelers at local baking supply stores and online.

- If you like the principle of the alternative method but find the toothpicks irksome, you can remove them and just use the holes as a visual guideline.

Filling a Cake

Fillings add flavor, and the multiple layers that fillings require add elegance to a cake. All of the cakes featured in this book are layer cakes. Fillings, and the flavor combinations they allow, are among the best features of a layer cake. Fillings don't have to be complicated or fancy. You can use the buttercream icing you already have on hand or, for added flavor, try using jam or chocolate–hazelnut spread.

Insert a coupler into a pastry bag (see Cutting a Bag, page 42) and fill the bag with icing. Holding the bag nearly vertical, pipe a ring of icing around the outer edge on top of a cake layer.

Continue to pipe concentric icing circles into the center until the top of the cake layer is completely covered.

Use a small offset spatula to smooth the seams. You want the filling to be level and flat, but don't concern yourself greatly with making it ultra-smooth.

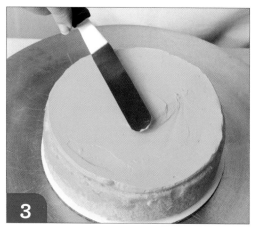

Set another cake layer on top of the filling, making sure the top layer is centered over the bottom layer.

Bits & Nibbles

- How close you hold the bag to the cake will dictate how much filling you add. If you're crazy for icing, hold the bag a full ½ inch (1 cm) from the surface of the cake and allow the coupler to unfurl icing the full width of its diameter. If you prefer less filling, hold the bag so that the coupler is just above the surface of the cake. The standard filling height for buttercream and other similar icings is ¼ to ⅓ inch (5 to 8 mm) thick.

- If you plan on filling a cake with a slippery jam or a thin curd, you'll want to create a dam to ensure that the filling doesn't leak and the layers don't slide. To make a dam, follow step 1 to create a ring of icing, then fill the ring with your selected filling.

Crumb-Coating a Cake

If you take away one nugget of information from this book, let it be the importance of the crumb coating. Enthusiastic home bakers are frequently discouraged by crumbs that lift away from the cake in continent-sized sheets, turning smooth buttercream into lumpy spackle. A thin, fast coat of icing and 15 minutes in the fridge will trap those pesky crumbs and set you up for icing success.

Slip a cardboard round under a cooled, crowned and filled cake and set the cake in the center of the turntable. Using a straight or offset spatula, begin to coat the sides of the cake with a thin layer of icing.

Continue to add icing to the top and sides of the cake, without concern for straying crumbs.

3

Once the cake is fully coated, use the spatula and the rotation of the turntable to scrape off excess icing so that only a thin layer remains.

4

Clean excess icing off the surface of the turntable. Place the cake, still on the turntable, in the refrigerator for about 15 minutes, until the crumb coating is thoroughly chilled, before you begin icing the cake.

Bits & Nibbles

- A layer cake on top of a turntable is a bulky affair and can take up a good amount of space in the fridge. Before you begin crumb-coating the cake, clear space in the fridge and double-check height requirements to ensure you don't lop off the top of your cake when placing it in the fridge.

- Many turntable surfaces are not permanently affixed to their bases, so you should never pick up a turntable from the top. Always lift it securely by the base; otherwise, a cracked tile or toenail could result.

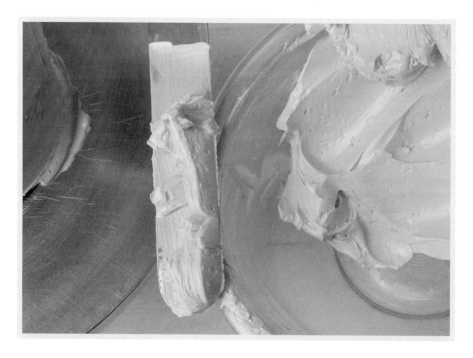

Transferring a Cake

Once the cake is iced (see chapter 4 for various icing techniques), you will need to move it from the turntable onto the presentation surface. The method is simple, but it does take mustering a bit of courage to balance your lovingly iced cake on one hand.

Prepare the presentation surface by using a squeeze bottle to dribble corn syrup over the area where the cake will rest.

Slide the tip of a large offset spatula underneath the cardboard round that sits beneath the cake.

Gently wiggle the spatula far enough underneath that you can lift the near edge of the cake and fit your fingers beneath it.

Keeping the spatula in place and using it to help balance the cake, almost as if it were a second hand, lift the cake from the turntable.

Center the cake over the presentation surface and set the back edge of the cake down.

Slip your fingers out from underneath the cake, then use the spatula to lower the front edge of the cake onto the presentation surface. Gently slide or wiggle the spatula out, leaving the cake in place.

Bits & Nibbles

- Before transferring the cake, make sure the turntable is clean of excess icing and the seal has been broken between the icing and the turntable. To do this, rest the large, flat part of an offset spatula on the turntable, near the side edge of the cake. Slide just the middle portion of the long, thin edge ¼ inch (5 mm) under the icing. Keeping the spatula in place, rotate the turntable to break the icing seal.

- When working your fingers underneath the cake and setting the cake down on the presentation surface, tilt the cake the slightest amount possible so as to not damage the back edge of the cake.

- If the cake isn't quite centered after you have placed it on the presentation surface, you can shift it into the correct position before removing the spatula. If you have already removed the spatula, use the tip of the spatula to carefully push the thin edge of the cardboard round until the cake is centered.

Preparing the Pastry Bag
Cutting a Bag

A new pastry bag, whether plastic or fabric, tapers into a point with no hole at the end. It's up to you to determine its use and cut the hole to fit your needs. For the projects in this book, you will cut the bag to fit either a standard-size coupler or a large decorating tip that requires no coupler. Either way, be very careful not to cut the hole too big. A hole that is too big renders the bag practically useless.

A coupler consist of two parts: a conical coupler base and a coupler ring. Before you begin, disassemble the coupler into its two parts, setting the ring aside.

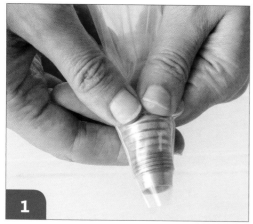

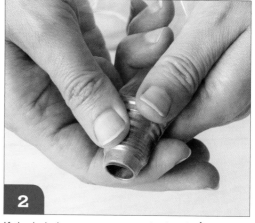

Use scissors to cut no more than ½ inch (1 cm) off the tip of the bag. Insert the coupler base or tip into the bag, narrow side down, to see if it fits.

If the hole is too narrow, cut the bag in ⅛-inch (3 mm) increments until the coupler base or tip fits snugly in the hole with about half of its length extending beyond the bag.

Bits & Nibbles

- Plastic and fabric bags alike have different rates of stretch and give. A plastic bag tends to stretch more than fabric. In either case, the hole should be cut so that only half of the coupler base or decorating tip pokes through. This allows a margin of grace should the bag continue to stretch with use.

- When you're cutting a hole in a pastry bag, it can go from too narrow to gaping and ruined in an instant. After the initial cut, snip just a fraction off the end at a time until the coupler base or tip fits snugly inside.

- Try to cut the bag perfectly straight. If it is cut on a bias, the coupler or tip will rest in the bag at an angle, making decorating a tad trickier.

Attaching a Decorating Tip

You could certainly drop a decorating tip into a bag without using a coupler, but a coupler gives you the ability to switch between tips without preparing a whole new bag, which adds up to less time, less waste and less cleanup. Couplers are a standardized size and should accommodate any standard-size tip.

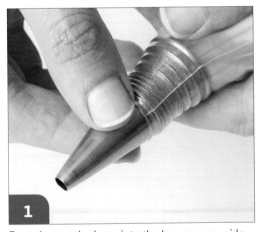

Drop the coupler base into the bag, narrow side down, ensuring that a few of its threads extend past the end of the bag. Place the decorating tip onto the end of the coupler.

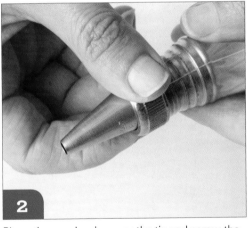

Place the coupler ring over the tip and screw the ring onto the coupler base.

Filling a Bag

There are many ways to fill a pastry bag. If I'm working with a large bowl of buttercream icing, I will just roll the top of the bag over the top of my hand, take a scoop from the top of the bowl and place it in the bag. But this only works if the bowl is big enough and full enough to weigh itself down and stay in place while you scoop.

Often, you need just a small amount of colored icing, and you need to scrape every last bit of it from the bowl, a task that requires two hands. Here's an easy way to avoid chasing the bowl around the counter with one hand:

1. Take a pastry bag fitted with the requisite tip and fold the top down about a third of the way.
2. Insert the bottom of the bag into an empty jar or drinking glass, making sure that the fold edge falls outside the jar and the opening is neat and wide. (Adjust the size of the jar or glass to the size of the bag: a bigger bag calls for a bigger jar or glass.)
3. Use a rubber spatula to scoop icing into the bag.

Preparing Icing Colors
Color Theory

Part intuition and part science, with results completely predictable and entirely surprising, color mixing can be one of the most creative and satisfying aspects of cake decorating. Understanding a few basic color theory concepts will allow you to transform a few bottles of mundane colors into an unlimited palette of nuance and style.

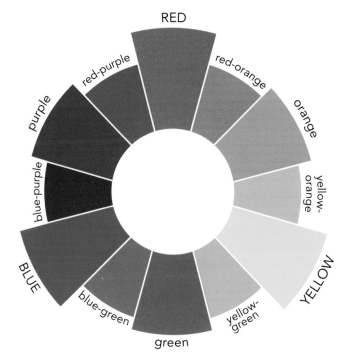

Primary Colors

There are three primary colors: red, yellow and blue. Incredibly, these pure hues can combine to create any color. These three colors are also the only hues that cannot be created by mixing other colors together. Think of them as the origin of the species, the parents of all the colors that follow.

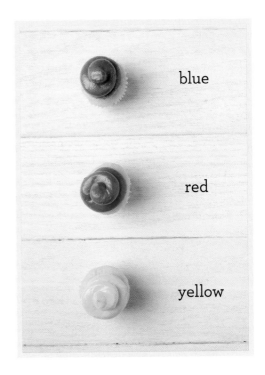

blue

red

yellow

Secondary Colors

Secondary colors are the result of two primary colors being mixed together. Depending on which two parents are combined, there are three potential progenies: purple, orange or green.

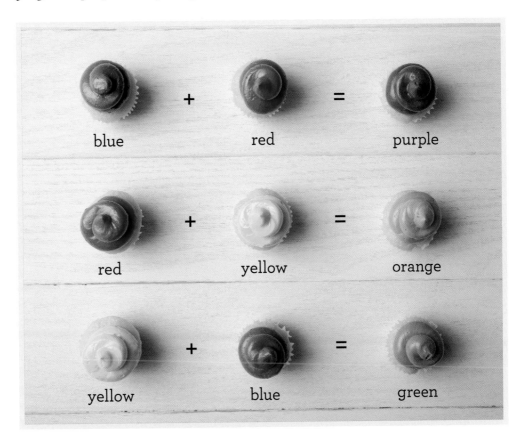

blue + red = purple

red + yellow = orange

yellow + blue = green

Tertiary Colors

Tertiary colors are created when you mix a primary color with its nearest secondary color on the color wheel. The six grandchildren that result are: yellow-orange, red-orange, red-purple, blue-purple, blue-green and yellow-green.

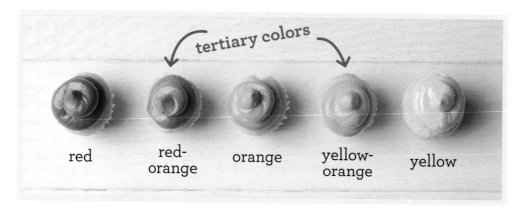

The primary, secondary and tertiary hues make up the 12 basic colors and are your gateway to every color imaginable. Because food coloring does not use pure hues, it's not possible to mix saturated jewel tones from the three primary colors alone. Mixing red and blue food coloring together will result in a muddy hue only vaguely reminiscent of purple. I recommend purchasing, at a minimum, the six primary and secondary colors, black and any of the tertiary colors that strike your fancy.

Uncolored buttercream icing plays the role of white food coloring. When getting ready to decorate, reserve a portion of uncolored icing to use exclusively for mixing and softening colors.

Complementary Colors

Complementary colors are two colors that sit directly across from one another on the color wheel. Complementary color sets include, but are not limited to: red and green, yellow and purple; blue and orange.

Sample Complementary Colors

Complementary colors are essential to decorating for two reasons. First, if you put a color next to its complement, both colors will pop brightly. If you're looking to make a statement, or to add drama or contrast to your cake, then decorate using two complementary colors.

Complementary colors placed side by side may pop, but mix the two colors together and they neutralize one another, and this is the second reason complementary colors are vital to decorating. Learning to neutralize colors from their original, straight-from-the-bottle Day-Glo hue is indispensable for creating sophisticated and nuanced color palettes. Adding black can also neutralize color, but with a flattening effect. Adding a touch of a color's complement will dull the brightness slightly without completely changing the color. Continue to add more of the complement and your color will neutralize further, eventually becoming an interesting brown or gray.

Bits & Nibbles

- To practice using complementary colors, decorate an elegant Christmas cake with a refined color palette by adding a touch of green to the red and a smidgen of the red into the green.

- To decorate a cake in pastels that doesn't look like it was shipped express from the Easter Bunny, add a bit of the complementary color to each pastel.

Adding Color to Buttercream

Now that you know the basics of color theory, you'll be using multiple colors and sizable quantities of food coloring to create interesting color palettes. Forgo the little plastic jars of color in favor of convenient squeeze bottles. Squeeze bottles allow you to quickly and easily add color with one hand, without fussing with multiple lids and dozens of toothpicks.

Below are step-by-step directions for coloring green buttercream. Note how many colors and how much food coloring are used to make this common and natural-looking leaf green. The addition of purple neutralizes and dulls the green. The orange further neutralizes the green, but also gives it some life.

The more you experiment and practice, the more you will be able to intuit what colors to mix, and in what proportions, to achieve your desired hue.

Place uncolored icing in a bowl and squeeze in a generous amount of leaf green food coloring.

Mix in the color with a rubber spatula and determine whether you need to add more green food coloring.

Add several drops of purple food coloring to the icing and stir.

Add several drops of orange food coloring to the icing and stir.

Take a step back and analyze the color you have created. If the color is too light, add more green. If it is too dark, add more white icing. If it is too bright, add more purple or add the complement of green, red. If the green is overly dull and lifeless, add lemon yellow to perk it up.

Bits & Nibbles

- You can purchase smaller squeeze bottles of food coloring than what is pictured here. Your local craft store may not carry them, but you can purchase them online or at bakery supply stores. If the bottles are closed tightly in between decorating sessions, food coloring can keep for years.

- Buttercream icing can absorb a surprising quantity of food coloring. You should be able to mix even the most saturated jewel tones without the buttercream separating.

- Colored buttercream, especially darker colors, will intensify and become more saturated as it sits and is exposed to air. If you are looking to match a specific color palette, it might be worth mixing the colors the night before to see how they transform.

Striping a Pastry Bag

To stripe a pastry bag means to add a small amount of a second color, or even two additional colors, to the bag. This little bit of extra color really contributes to the dynamic energy of the decoration being piped. Subtle color shifts add nuance and interest, shadow and light, and make for a more naturalistic appearance.

Prepare the dominant color and one or two supporting colors.

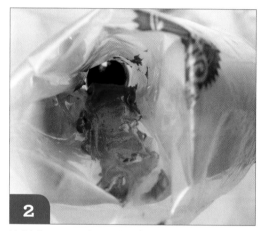

Hold the pastry bag with the top folded over your hand, creating a wide opening. Use a spatula to scoop up a small amount of the first supporting color and spread it vertically along one side of the bag.

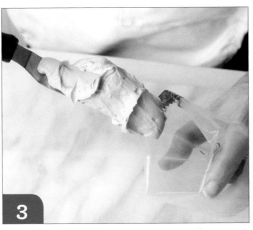

3 If using a second supporting color, use the spatula to scoop up that color and make another vertical stripe inside the bag.

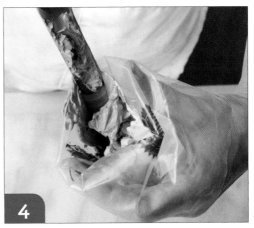

4 Finish filling the bag with the dominant color.

Bits & Nibbles

- The dominant color should fill the majority of the bag.

- An easy way to stripe a bag without spending time mixing extra colors is to stripe it with white icing.

- For a subtle, elegant effect, stripe a bag with two or three shades of the same color.

Preparing to Decorate

The miraculous coordination between what the eye sees and what the hand feels is conveyed here in writing and pictures, yet mere words and two-dimensional photographs can be inadequate when describing an act that occurs on multiple planes and dimensions. Although I can't be with you to adjust the angle of the bag or the position of the tip, I've put together a set of definitions that will help us speak the same language when describing this multifaceted act of creativity.

Bag Angle

Bag angle refers to the slant of the pastry bag in relation to the surface of the cake, turntable or rose nail. The angle of the bag determines how the buttercream icing will flow through the tip, whether it will curve or pile up. Most of the techniques call for the bag to be held vertical, or nearly so, or to be held at a 45-degree angle, halfway between vertical and horizontal.

Bag Direction

Think of the top of the cake as the face of a clock and the pastry bag as the hour hand. When the bag is held in the 6 o'clock direction, the tip of the bag faces the center of the cake and the base of the bag points to 6 o'clock. The tip could be at the center of the cake or at the near or far edge; what's important is that the tip and bag are kept aligned with 6 o'clock.

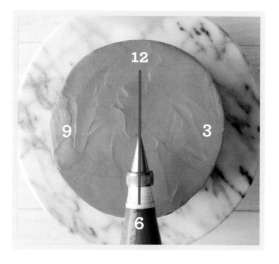

Bag direction and bag angle work together, so a bag might be held at a 45-degree angle in the 3 o'clock direction.

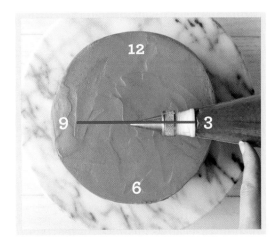

Starting Position

Starting position refers to the point on the cake where the tip of the pastry bag (or a spatula or comb) is placed to start the decoration. The points of a compass are used to distinguish the starting position from the bag direction. When a cake is placed in front of you, north (N) is the farthest edge, directly across from you, south (S) is directly in front of you, east (E) is the edge on the right side of the cake and west (W) is on the left.

Here, the starting point is the northwest (NW) position:

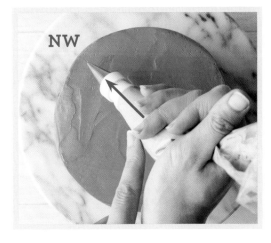

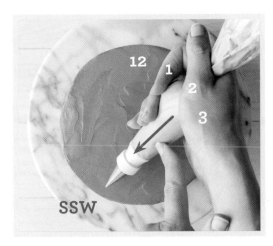

Bag angle, bag direction and starting position can be combined to give you precise direction on where and how to start decorating. For example, this bag is held at a 45-degree angle, in the 2 o'clock direction, with the tip at the south-southwest (SSW) position.

Tip Position

Tip position refers to the position of the tip in relation to the surface of the cake. The tip can be held just above the surface of the cake or lightly touching it. It can be 1/8 inch (3 mm) from the surface or as much as 1/2 inch (1 cm) away. Here, the tip is just touching the surface of the cake.

For tips with asymmetrical openings, such as a petal or rose tip, tip position also tells you how to orient the opening.

Pressure and Speed

Pressure refers to how much force is applied to squeeze the icing out of the bag. The pressure applied determines how fast the icing is released, which affects the uniformity and consistency of the decoration. Pressure can be gentle, moderate or firm.

In most cases, the speed with which you move the bag to complete a motion should match the pressure applied to the bag: gentle pressure is paired with slow movement, moderate pressure with medium speed, and firm pressure with quicker movement. Matching pressure and speed will result in a consistent stream of icing.

The Effects of Pressure and Speed

1. Matching and consistent speed and pressure.
2. Fast speed and gentle pressure, resulting in a broken line of icing.
3. Slow speed and moderate pressure, resulting in a thick, wavering line.
4. Slow speed and firm pressure, resulting in the line curling and backing up.

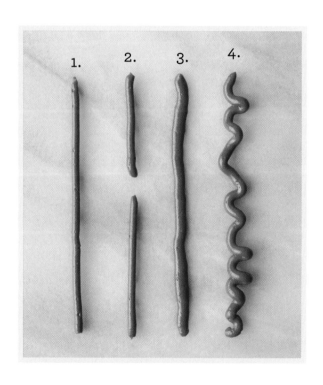

Notes for Left-Handers

The step-by-step instructions in this book are written for those who are right-handed, but they can be easily adapted for those who are left-handed by making these adjustments.

- *Bag direction:* If the instructions tell you to hold the bag in a direction on the right side of the clock, switch to holding the bag in a corresponding direction on the left side of the clock. For example, if they say to hold the bag in the 3 o'clock direction, you should hold the bag in the 9 o'clock direction. If they say to hold the bag in the 2 o'clock direction, you should hold it in the 10 o'clock direction.

- *Starting position:* If the instructions tell you to hold the bag with the tip at a point on the right side of the compass, switch to holding the bag at a corresponding point on the left side of the compass. For example, if they say to hold the bag with the tip in the southwest (SW) position, you should hold it with the tip in the southeast (SE) position.

- *Turntable rotation:* For actions that are performed while you simultaneously rotate the turntable, you should rotate it in the opposite of the direction specified. For example, if the directions say to squeeze the pastry bag with firm pressure while spinning the turntable clockwise, you should spin the turntable counterclockwise.

Chapter 4
The Icing on the Cake

The icing on the cake doesn't just set the stage for buttercream decoration, it is a thing of beauty in its own right. A simply frosted cake displays the best qualities of buttercream.

Cakes meant for decorating are customarily iced with a smooth, polished finish; although pristine, a smooth finish doesn't begin to visually convey the phenomenon of texture and taste that Swiss buttercream offers. Think of the icing on the cake not simply as the opening act for decoration but as an entire show, complete with plot, action, climax and resolution.

Cake decorating is an amazing act of creativity and celebration, but sometimes you just want to eat cake. When you do, try one of these sumptuous finishes to present your cake with simple, classic elegance.

Modern Vintage

Historically, the best cakes came from grandmothers' kitchens, when cake recipes were traded like baseball cards and cake mix from a box wasn't an option. Grandma iced cakes with a charming homespun nonchalance that's difficult to replicate. I've taken what I learned from Grandma and added a contemporary bent, and I've broken down icing a cake into a series of manageable steps. Whether you're desperate for cake, quickly iced, as a midweek mood enhancer or are creating a base for a highly decorated masterpiece, one of these four modern vintage styles will suit the occasion splendidly.

Project 1: Polished

The ability to give an iced cake a smooth, polished finish is an indispensable skill. Smooth icing is the foundation for all other icing styles and textures, and is the primary platform on which to decorate.

Cake: Any size cake

Buttercream: 4 cups (1 L) for a 6-inch (15 cm) cake; 5 cups (1.25 L) for an 8-inch (20 cm) cake; 6 cups (1.5 L) for a 10-inch (25 cm) cake

Other Stuff: Straight spatula
Triangular comb
Large rectangular comb with a straight edge (or bench scraper with a 90-degree angle that can sit flush with the top of the turntable)
Large offset spatula
Damp kitchen towel

Cake Prep: Crumb-coat and chill the cake, then place it in the center of the turntable.

Decorating Steps

1

Drop a large mound of buttercream in the center of the cake.

2

Rotating the turntable clockwise, use the straight spatula to spread the icing out from the center to the edge, distributing it evenly across the cake. It should be about $1/3$ inch (8 mm) thick.

3

Hold the spatula on the right side on top of the cake, with the back edge lightly touching the icing and the front edge raised to a 45-degree angle. Spin the turntable counterclockwise, applying light pressure with the spatula to smooth the surface.

4

Allow the icing to reach past the edges of the cake, forming a ledge.

5

Still using the straight spatula, lift small mounds of buttercream from the bowl and distribute them around the sides of the cake, roughly smoothing the icing as you go.

6

Continue spreading icing over the sides of the cake until the cake is fully covered and the icing is about $1/3$ inch (8 mm) thick.

Phraseology

Roughly Iced: For many icing techniques and finishes (including most of the projects in this chapter), an underlayer of smooth perfection is not required. Rough icing is thicker and more precise than a crumb coating, but not as fussy and formal as smooth icing. A cake that has been roughly iced has straight sides and a ¼-inch (5 mm) layer of icing, but has not been smoothed to an immaculate finish. To roughly ice a cake, follow steps 1 to 8, 11 and 12 of Polished.

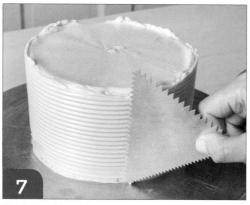

7 Hold any side of the triangular comb vertically at the south-southwest (SSW) position on the side of the cake. Tilt the point of the comb forward to a 45-degree angle. Spin the turntable clockwise through a couple of rotations.

8 Look for holes, gaps or an absence of lines on the sides of the cake. Using the tip of the spatula, spread just enough icing over the flaws to cover them. Don't worry if the added icing isn't very smooth.

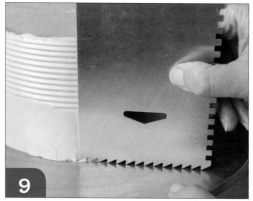

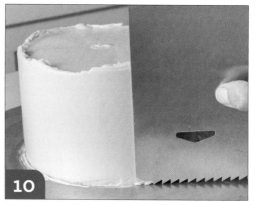

9 Hold the straight edge of the rectangular comb vertically at SSW on the side of the cake. Tilt the left edge of the comb forward to a 45-degree angle. Start spinning the turntable clockwise.

10 Continue to spin the turntable until the icing is smooth, the sides are vertical and there is a lip of icing all the way around the top edge of the cake.

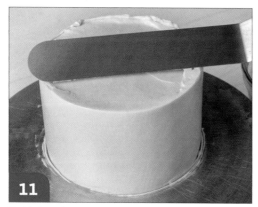

11 Hold the offset spatula horizontally in midair just in front of the southwest (SW) position at the top edge of the cake. Tilt the right edge up to a 45-degree angle. Touch the back edge of the spatula to the lip of icing and drag the icing toward the center, simultaneously lifting it off the cake.

12 Rotate the turntable slightly and repeat step 11, removing the lip in segments, until the entire lip is removed and there is a clean 90-degree angle between the sides and top of the cake. Clean the spatula on the rim of the icing bowl between each swipe.

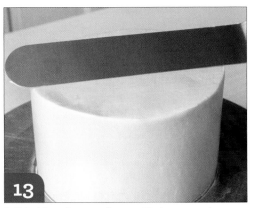

13

Still holding the spatula at a 45-degree angle, very lightly drag the back edge from the SW position across the top of the cake toward the northeast (NE) position, smoothing any unevenness. Raise the spatula just before it reaches NE.

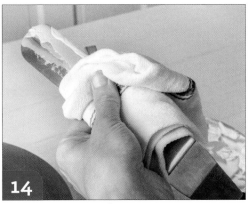

14

Use a damp towel to clean any icing off the spatula between swipes. Repeat step 13, rotating the turntable slightly between swipes, until the top of the cake is smooth and even.

Bits & Nibbles

- When you're smoothing the top of the cake in step 3, the spatula will scrape off a thin layer of icing. Clean the spatula as necessary by scraping it across the rim of the icing bowl.

- In step 7, the horizontal impressions created by the triangular comb help you see where more icing is needed, so you can create a straight vertical surface on the sides of the cake. Try to scrape off as little icing as possible in this step.

- Although you will inevitably lift some icing from the sides of the cake in steps 9 and 10, try to remove as little as possible. These steps are for pushing and smoothing, not for leveling or evening out. Clean the comb frequently on the rim of the icing bowl to ensure that the lifted icing is not redistributed over the cake (which would make it difficult to smooth).

- When you're removing the lip of icing in steps 11 and 12, try not to redistribute the icing over the top of the cake. Use a light but confident hand to drag and lift it up off the cake.

- The final smoothing in steps 13 and 14 should be executed with finesse and a light touch, removing a minimal amount of icing.

- A cake that looks "right" doesn't just have a smooth surface; it also has vertical sides. Aim for a 90-degree angle between the sides and top of the cake.

- When you're finished, the icing on the cake should be about $\frac{1}{4}$ inch (5 mm) thick. You may be wondering how to visually determine its thickness. You can't — at least, not without a well-practiced eye or serious icing experience under your belt. In the meantime, just poke in the tip of a straight spatula just before the final smooth.

Project 2: Lath and Plaster

Use this forgiving finish in place of the finicky smoothness of Polished (page 59). The surface is still even enough for most decorating projects.

Cake: Any size cake, crumb-coated and chilled

Buttercream: 4 cups (1 L) for a 6-inch (15 cm) cake; 5 cups (1.25 L) for an 8-inch (20 cm) cake; 6 cups (1.5 L) for a 10-inch (25 cm) cake

Other Stuff: Straight spatula

Cake Prep: Roughly ice the cake (see Phraseology, page 61).

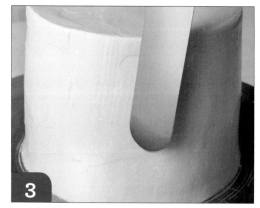

Reaching over the top of the cake at the southwest (SW) position, hold the spatula so that a side edge of the rounded tip is at a 45-degree angle toward you on the side of the cake.

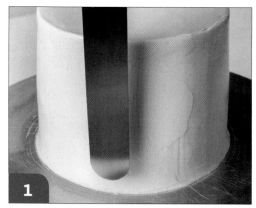

Moving the spatula toward you, swipe a shallow, irregular impression onto the side of the cake.

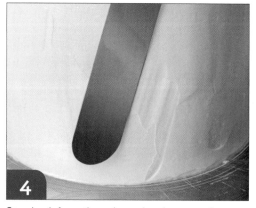

Continue to make scattered impressions, in random places and in arbitrary directions, through one full rotation of the turntable, moving your hand up or down between swipes to avoid uniformity and regular spacing.

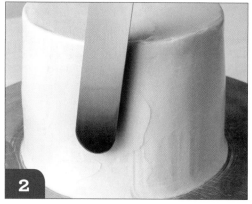

Step back from the cake and make note of any areas that remain smooth. Reach over the cake again and, reversing the angle of the spatula, make random swipes in the opposite direction to fill in any gaps.

5

Holding a side edge of the spatula at a 45-degree angle to the top of the cake, swipe random shallow impressions over the top of the cake until it is completely covered with an irregular pattern.

Piece of Cake

Think your iced cake looks a little plain? Or perhaps you're not wholly satisfied with your icing efforts? The answer is always sprinkles. Add sprinkles just for kicks and giggles or to hide any icing blemishes.

Bits & Nibbles

- Use a damp kitchen towel to clean the icing off your spatula in between swipes.

- When making impressions on the side of the cake, you should be using only a 1- to 2-inch (2.5 to 5 cm) portion of the spatula.

- In steps 3 and 4, change the direction and placement of your impressions with each swipe, moving right, left, up, down and on a diagonal, until the sides of the cake are completely covered with an irregular pattern. In step 3 keep your swipes going in a generally forward direction (toward you), and in step 4 keep them going in a generally backward direction (away from you) so that you're not fighting against the angle of the spatula and digging into the icing.

- In step 5, start some swipes at the edge of the cake and some in the middle, and alter the direction of your swipes often, sometimes swiping toward you and sometimes away from you. Remember to rotate the turntable slightly between swipes.

Project 3: Coiled Rustic

The trendy rustic finish is simple to execute and is both interesting and neutral enough to display any topper.

Cake: Any size cake, crumb-coated and chilled

Buttercream: 4 cups (1 L) for a 6-inch (15 cm) cake; 5 cups (1.25 L) for an 8-inch (20 cm) cake; 6 cups (1.5 L) for a 10-inch (25 cm) cake

Other Stuff: Straight spatula

Cake Prep: Roughly ice the cake (see Phraseology, page 61).

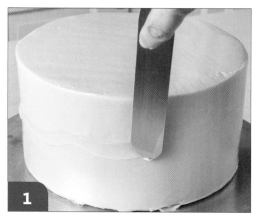

Reaching over the top of the cake at the southwest (SW) position, hold the spatula so that a side edge of the rounded tip is at a 45-degree angle to the side of the cake. Swipe a shallow, thin and narrow smile shape.

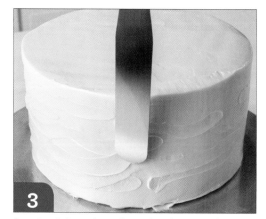

Swipe smile and frown shapes around the sides of the cake, rotating the turntable between each swipe and moving your hand up or down between swipes to avoid uniformity and regular spacing.

Step back from the cake and make note of any areas that remain smooth. Reach over the cake again and fill in any gaps until the sides of the cake are completely covered with an irregular pattern.

Holding the rounded tip of the spatula at a 45-degree angle to the top of the cake, swipe smiles and frowns over the top of the cake until it is completely covered with an irregular pattern.

Bits & Nibbles

- Use a damp kitchen towel to clean the icing off your spatula in between swipes.

- When making impressions on the side of the cake, you should be using only a ½- to 1-inch (1 to 2.5 cm) portion of the spatula.

- In addition to the smiles and frowns, you can add long, undulating impressions by slowly rotating the turntable while moving your hand in a rhythmic up-and-down motion.

Project 4: Vintage Homestyle

Use this swoopy updated version of Grandma's showpiece when you need a nifty iced cake without decorations.

Cake: Any size cake, crumb-coated and chilled

Buttercream: 4 cups (1 L) for a 6-inch (15 cm) cake; 5 cups (1.25 L) for an 8-inch (20 cm) cake; 6 cups (1.5 L) for a 10-inch (25 cm) cake

Other Stuff: Straight spatula

Cake Prep: Roughly ice the cake (see Phraseology, page 61).

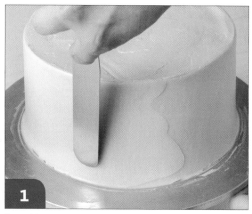

Reaching over the top of the cake at the southwest (SW) position, hold the spatula so that a side edge of the rounded tip is at a 45-degree angle to the side of the cake. Swipe a shallow, fat swoop in any direction.

Swipe swoops in all directions around the sides of the cake, rotating the turntable between each swipe and moving your hand up or down between swipes to avoid uniformity and regular spacing.

Step back from the cake and make note of any areas that remain smooth. Reach over the cake again and fill in any gaps until the sides of the cake are completely covered with an irregular pattern.

Holding the rounded tip of the spatula at a 45-degree angle to the top of the cake, swipe fat swoops over the top of the cake until it is completely covered with an irregular pattern.

Cake Debate

Q: Dear Carey, I don't know what I was thinking. In a moment of unprecedented confidence and, doubtless, temporary insanity, I agreed to make my friend's wedding cake. Yikes! I'm pretty confident in my baking abilities, but my legs are shaking in their kitchen clogs when I think about decorating. I love the look of a fondant-covered cake, but I'm making this one with organic, local, sustainably harvested ingredients, and I'm not enthusiastic about the idea of draping it with a substance reminiscent of Silly Putty. At the same time, I've never been able to achieve a perfectly smooth, flawlessly iced cake. Please advise.

Sincerely, Aspiring Smooth Operator

A: Dear ASO, I applaud your courage and willingness to stretch beyond your comfort zone. Keep in mind that perfection is not the goal. Your offering of labor and love is of greater value to your dear friend than any immaculate bakery cake. I do not discount the beauty of a cake covered with fondant, but being labeled "edible" does not a food make, nor does "nontoxic" equate to an enjoyable eating experience. Lay your fears to rest and ditch the flawed premise that an elegant, well-iced cake must be pristinely smooth. Instead, aspire for a surface that is slightly textured and appreciate the sensuous, imperfect beauty and real food quality of buttercream icing.

Bits & Nibbles

- Use a damp kitchen towel to clean the icing off your spatula in between swipes.

- Don't be stingy with the icing on this cake. You want plenty of depth for making luscious swoops and to avoid gouging the cake.

- Don't overthink or become overly precious with his icing technique — Grandma never did. Loosen up, maybe put on a snappy tune and swoop it up.

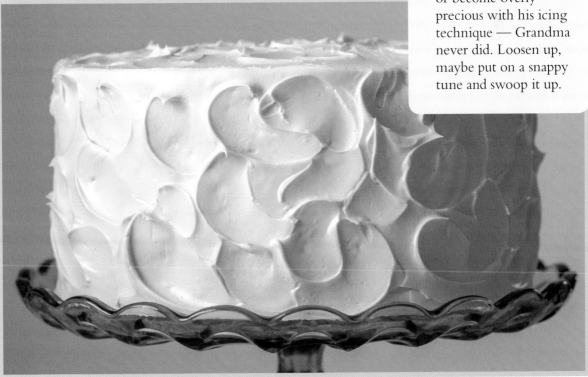

Spellbound

Minimalistic and straightforward, these cakes are contemporary without taking themselves too seriously. If cakes were people, these two would be my bosom buddies. Something about their swirling pattern makes them lighthearted and fun, and the climbing spirals make them particularly forgiving of icing imperfections.

Project 1: Spiral

Cake: Any size cake, crumb-coated and chilled

Buttercream: 4 cups (1 L) for a 6-inch (15 cm) cake; 5 cups (1.25 L) for an 8-inch (20 cm) cake; 6 cups (1.5 L) for a 10-inch (25 cm) cake

Other Stuff: Straight spatula

Cake Prep: Roughly ice the cake (see Phraseology, page 61).

Decorating Steps

1 Hold a side edge of the spatula nearly parallel to the turntable at the south (S) position. Place the rounded tip of the spatula flat against the cake and the bottom edge of the tip on the turntable.

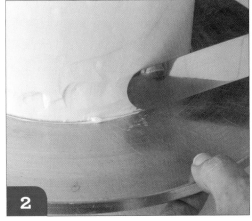

2 Hold the spatula steady and unmoving as you apply light pressure and rotate the turntable clockwise until a shallow groove encircles the bottom of the cake.

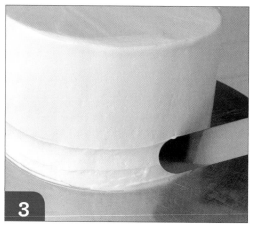

3

4

As you near the end of the first rotation, slowly draw the spatula up just above the first groove and make a second groove around the cake.

Continue to rotate at a measured pace until the grooves spiral all the way to the top of the cake.

5

6

Holding the tip of the spatula at a 45-degree angle to the top of the cake, place it at the southwest (SW) position, near the edge. Hold the spatula steady as you apply light pressure and rotate the turntable clockwise.

Lightly draw the spatula in toward the center as you complete each rotation, until the spiral reaches the center of the cake.

Bits & Nibbles

- Don't waste time being overly finicky about getting the spiraled lines just right. Take a deep breath, close your eyes and just go. Well, you want to keep your eyes open, but as long as the spatula doesn't dig into the cake, it's going to look awesome.

- Don't worry if there's space in between the grooves or if they overlap. It will not detract from the appearance of the cake.

Piece of Cake

If you feel nervous about attempting a spiral on the vertical side of the cake, you can skip steps 1 to 4 and just make a spiral on top of the cake.

Project 2: Twine

Cake: Any size cake, crumb-coated and chilled

Buttercream: 4 cups (1 L) for a 6-inch (15 cm) cake; 5 cups (1.25 L) for an 8-inch (20 cm) cake; 6 cups (1.5 L) for a 10-inch (25 cm) cake

Other Stuff: Small tapered offset spatula
Straight spatula

Cake Prep: Roughly ice the cake (see Phraseology, page 61).

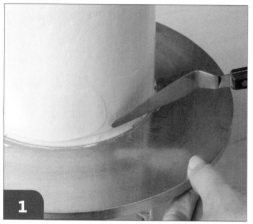

1 Hold the offset spatula facing you and place the bottom edge nearly parallel to the turntable at the south (S) position. Place the tip of the spatula flat against the cake, near the base.

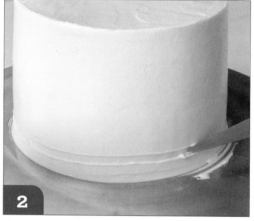

2 Hold the spatula steady and unmoving as you apply light pressure and rotate the turntable clockwise until a thin, shallow gully encircles the bottom of the cake.

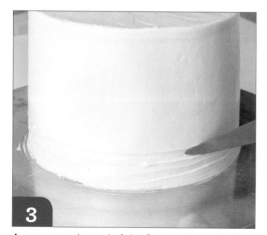

3 As you near the end of the first rotation, slowly draw the spatula up just above the first gully and make a second gully around the cake.

4 Continue to rotate at a measured pace until the gullies spiral all the way to the top of the cake.

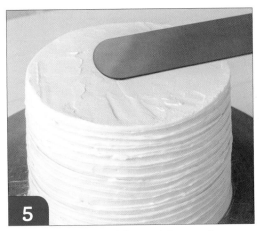

5

Holding a side edge of the straight spatula at a 45-degree angle to the top of the cake, swipe random shallow impressions over the top of the cake until it is completely covered with an irregular pattern.

Up Your Game

Continue the spiral pattern on top of the cake by following steps 5 and 6 of Spiral (page 72), but still using the tapered offset spatula.

Bits & Nibbles

- Use a damp kitchen towel to clean the icing off your spatula occasionally, then start again where you left off.

- Don't worry if there's space in between the grooves or if they overlap or undulate. It will not detract from the appearance of the cake.

- In step 5, start some swipes at the edge of the cake and some in the middle, and alter the direction of your swipes often, sometimes swiping toward you and sometimes away from you. Remember to rotate the turntable slightly between swipes.

Combed

For me, a traditionally combed cake brings to mind the hapless carnation, the dowdy stepsister of the rose. There's nothing inherently wrong with a carnation. On its own, it is a resplendent ruffled pompom of a blossom, but once paired with ferns and baby's breath and dyed a noxious blue, carnations start to resemble my puff-sleeved prom gown from 1992. Time-honored but tired, the combed cake is a grocery store bakery staple. But when iced in a saturated primary color or using an unconventional comb, it becomes something altogether new and provocative.

Cake: Any size cake, crumb-coated and chilled

Buttercream: 4 cups (1 L) for a 6-inch (15 cm) cake; 5 cups (1.25 L) for an 8-inch (20 cm) cake; 6 cups (1.5 L) for a 10-inch (25 cm) cake

Other Stuff: Triangular comb
Straight spatula

Cake Prep: Roughly ice the cake (see Phraseology, page 61).

Decorating Steps

1 Hold any side of the comb vertically at the south (S) position on the side of the cake. Tilt the point of the comb to a 45-degree angle toward the right side of the cake.

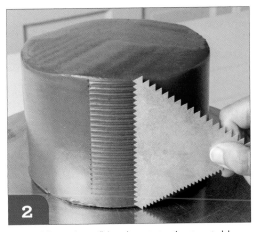

2 Smoothly and confidently rotate the turntable clockwise, dragging the tines of the comb through the icing to create a uniform ridged pattern.

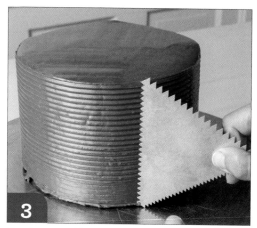

3 Continue combing through at least one full rotation, until the ridged pattern completely covers the sides of the cake.

4 If a lip of icing has formed around the top of the cake, use the spatula to remove it and smooth the surface (see steps 11 to 14 of Polished, pages 62–63).

Cake Debate

Q: Dear Carey, My combed cake looks like an old-school vinyl record with deep scratches. How do I get rid of the lines, skips and inconsistencies?

Thank You, One Warped Record

A: Dear OWR, Keep in mind that vinyl discs are spun and scratched by DJs. This technique takes confidence, so steady your hand and spin your turntable like the badass DJ you were born to be. Don't expect impeccability on the first rotation. Use multiple rotations and overlap the lines until you are satisfied. Just don't scrape off too much icing, and clean your comb between passes. Like the warm sound of classic vinyl, a combed cake might not be perfect, but it will be honest in its beauty.

Piece of Cake

Are you apprehensive about the whole notion of combing? Start off using a small-tined comb, such as the classic triangular comb, and work up to larger, wider-toothed combs. The multitudinous thin grooves made by small tines make it difficult for the eye to detect icing foibles.

Up Your Game

If the classic triangular comb has you feeling blasé, try one of the fun new shapes available, such as a sweet scallop comb or a comb that rakes only half the cake.

Cloud

Ditch the spatula and the comb, and forget about right angles and glossy smoothness. Instead, luxuriate in the ease and fluffy deliciousness of the Cloud. It's so simple to make and sweet to look at, and has the added possibility of upping your icing intake: just slice thin cake layers and make multiple cloud strata.

Cake: Any size cake

Pastry Bags: 1 bag, fitted with a coupler

Buttercream: 3 cups (750 mL) for a 6-inch (15 cm) cake; 4 cups (1 L) for an 8-inch (20 cm) cake; 5 cups (1.25 L) for a 10-inch (25 cm) cake

Other Stuff: ¼ cup (60 mL) unsweetened cocoa powder
Fine-mesh sieve

Bag Prep: Fill the pastry bag with icing.

Cake Prep: Slice the cake in half horizontally and center the bottom half on the presentation surface, securing it with a dribble of corn syrup. Place it in the center of the turntable.

Decorating Steps

1 Hold the pastry bag perpendicular to the top of the cake and ¼ to ½ inch (5 mm to 1 cm) above your starting point at the edge of the cake. Squeeze the bag with moderate pressure to create a fat dollop.

2 Rotate the turntable slightly and make another dollop next to the first. Continue to add dollops until you have made a full ring around the perimeter of the cake.

Create a second ring of dollops within the first. Continue to make increasingly smaller concentric rings until the top is completely covered with dollops.

Place the top half of the cake on top of the icing dollops, ensuring that the top and bottom cake halves are aligned. Press gently on the top to create a level surface.

Repeat steps 1 to 3 until the top of the cake is completely covered with dollops.

Place the cocoa powder in the sieve, center the sieve over the cake and tap gently on the rim until the cake is finely dusted with cocoa.

Bits & Nibbles

- Each time you make a dollop, release the pressure before moving the bag away.

- If your cake isn't chocolate, like the one shown here, scrap the dusting of cocoa powder and sprinkle your cake with something more appropriate, like nuts or sprinkles.

Fluted

A few flicks of the wrist and you have a cake that is both dynamic and elegant, with tremendous grace and movement. A fluted cake is ideal as a base for added decoration, but is also sublime on its own.

Cake: Any size cake, crumb-coated and chilled

Buttercream: 4 cups (1 L) for a 6-inch (15 cm) cake; 5 cups (1.25 L) for an 8-inch (20 cm) cake; 6 cups (1.5 L) for a 10-inch (25 cm) cake

Other Stuff: Straight spatula

Cake Prep: Roughly ice the cake (see Phraseology, page 61).

Decorating Steps

1. Hold a side edge of the spatula nearly parallel to the turntable at the south (S) position. Place the rounded tip of the spatula at a 45-degree angle to the cake and rest the bottom edge of the tip on the turntable.

2. Keeping the spatula parallel to the turntable and at a 45-degree angle to the cake, use determination and moderate pressure to drag the tip up through the icing past the top of the cake.

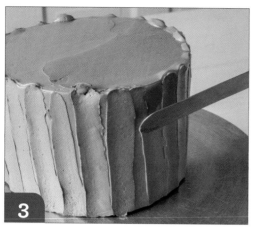

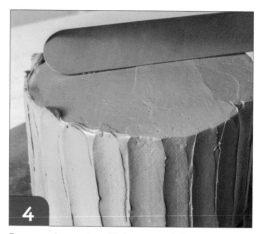

Rotating the turntable slightly between each swipe so that you start each channel at the south position, continue to swipe vertical channels, side by side, all the way around the cake.

Remove the peaks of icing around the top edge of the cake by following the instructions in steps 11 and 12 of Polished (page 62).

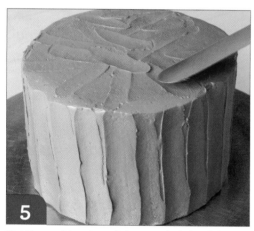

Holding a side edge of the rounded tip of the spatula at a 45-degree angle to the top of the cake, swipe random shallow impressions over the top of the cake until it is completely covered with an irregular pattern.

Up Your Game

Create diagonal channels by swiping up on a diagonal instead of straight up.

Bits & Nibbles

- When you're roughly icing the sides of this cake, make sure you don't use a light hand; if you do, you'll find it quite easy to reveal the surface of the cake as you swipe the channels.

- If your channels tend to narrow at the top, you're likely not swiping past the top of the cake. It's like carrying through with your swing after making contact with the ball in baseball or golf.

- Use a damp kitchen towel to clean the icing from the spatula after every few swipes.

- In step 5, start some swipes at the edge of the cake and some in the middle, and alter the direction of your swipes often, sometimes swiping toward you and sometimes away from you. Remember to rotate the turntable slightly between swipes.

Cake Debate

Q: Dear Carey, I love the look of fluted sides, but my channels are anemic and wobbly. Plus, they either overlap or there's too much space between them. Where is all that ease and dynamic movement you promised?

Sincerely, Wan and Wondering

A: Dear WAW, It's quite possible that there's such fantastic movement to this cake because there's an actual audible rhythm to making it. You could be overthinking the process and completely missing out on the musical merriment. No careful fussing is allowed while creating this confection. A true and steady hand that swipes with confidence is essential. You know you're in the zone when you hear a regularly timed tick each time the spatula strikes the turntable for another swipe. Getting into the rhythm will help you regularly space your channels.

Picnic

We've all had plenty of experience with wielding a fork, so even if you're unfamiliar with the basket-weave technique, you can be a fork decorating pro. This is a simple method for finishing a cake that requires no competency with a pastry bag and decorating tips.

Cake: Any size cake, crumb-coated and chilled

Buttercream: 4 cups (1 L) for a 6-inch (15 cm) cake; 5 cups (1.25 L) for an 8-inch (20 cm) cake; 6 cups (1.5 L) for a 10-inch (25 cm) cake

Other Stuff: 22, 28 or 34 inches (55, 70 or 85 cm) of ribbon (depending on cake size), neatly trimmed
Standard kitchen fork

Cake Prep: Ice the cake with a Polished finish (page 59) and center it on the presentation surface, securing it with a dribble of corn syrup. Chill the cake for 10 to 15 minutes, then place it in the center of the turntable and affix the ribbon around the bottom of the cake (see New Trick, page 90). Let the cake come to room temperature before starting step 1.

Piece of Cake

Let yourself off the hook by decorating only the sides of the cake. Leave the top smooth or lightly textured.

New Trick: Ribbon Border

To complete this technique, you will need a little bit of icing to glue the ends of the ribbon together. If you already have a pastry bag of icing loaded, you can pipe a dab of icing onto the ribbon; otherwise, you can just dab it on with the tip of your finger.

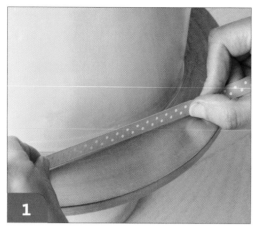

Stretch a short length of the ribbon, near one end, between your hands. Touch the middle portion of the ribbon length to the side of the cake, resting the bottom edge flush against the presentation surface.

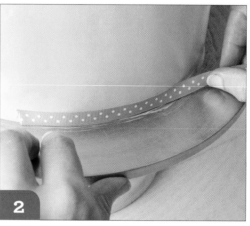

Working backward from the point where the ribbon makes contact with the cake, gently press along the ribbon until the loose end is affixed to the side of the cake.

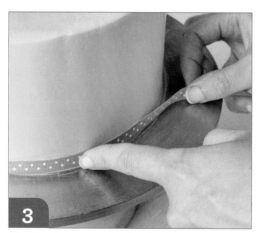

Working forward and using both hands in tandem, use one hand to pull and guide the remaining loose ribbon around the cake and the other to gently press the ribbon to the cake.

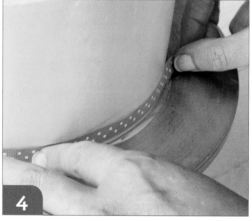

As you wrap and press the ribbon, run the pad of your index finger gently across it to smooth out any bubbles or creases.

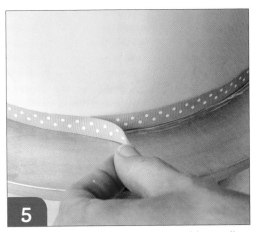

5

Continue guiding, pressing and smoothing until the ribbon is wrapped all the way around the cake. Trim excess ribbon, if necessary; there should be only enough ribbon remaining for a small amount of overlap.

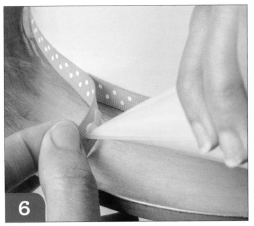

6

Use a small dab of icing to glue the overlapping end of the ribbon to the ribbon underneath so that it lies smooth.

Cake Debate

Q: Dear Carey, I have a busy life, and a decorated cake coming out of my kitchen is about as likely as me making time to iron my pillowcases with lavender-scented water, but I'd like to give it a shot. In the spirit of saving time, do I really need to chill the cake before applying a ribbon border?

Thanks, Giving It a Shot without Shooting Myself

A: Dear GIASWSM, I get where you're coming from, and the short answer is no, you do not need to chill the cake. You can apply a ribbon border on a room-temperature cake, but to safeguard against unintentional indentations in the icing, don't wrap the ribbon too tightly, or smooth with too much pressure. Chilling the cake for a mere 10 minutes will allow you a huge margin of error. If you place the ribbon too high, you can unwrap it and start over again; if it bumps up a smidge in one section, you can easily slide it down using a toothpick. It's completely up to you, but chilling the cake may save you valuable time in the long run. Good luck!

Decorating Steps

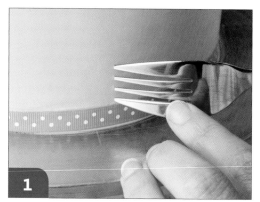

1

Turn the cake so that the ribbon overlap is at the South position. Holding the fork in your dominant hand and steadying the base with your other hand to allow for focused, even pressure, place the tines vertically just above the ribbon overlap.

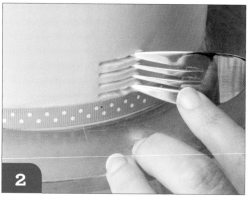

2

With the fork tilted forward at a 45-degree angle to the side of the cake, drag it toward you, making a set of horizontal indentations the same length as the width of the fork.

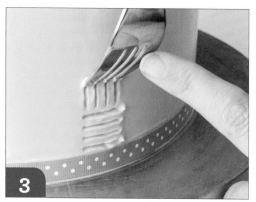

3

Turn the fork to face up, place the tines horizontally just above the first set of indentations, tilt the fork up to a 45-degree angle and drag it upward, making a square set of vertical indentations.

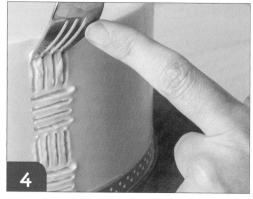

4

Alternate making horizontal and vertical sets of indentations until you have a column running up the side of the cake. Take a moment between every few swipes to clean excess icing off the fork tines with a damp kitchen towel.

5

Make a second column of alternating indentations directly next to the first, starting at the bottom with a set of vertical indentations.

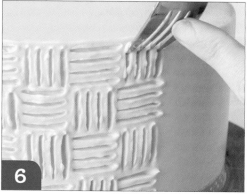

6

Continue until the sides of the cake are completely covered with columns of alternating indentations.

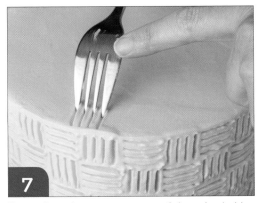

To continue the pattern on top of the cake, hold the fork facing down at one edge. Tilting the fork to a 45-degree angle, drag it toward the center of the cake to make your first set of indentations.

Continue to make sets of indentations in alternating directions until you have a row of indentations that bisects the cake.

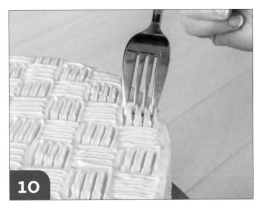

Working from the middle row toward the edges, continue to make rows of alternating indentations across the top of the cake.

As you work outward and the rows get shorter, make your starting and ending sets of indentations smaller, to line up evenly. Continue until the top of the cake is completely covered.

Bits & Nibbles

- If you have neared the top of a column and you cannot fit in a full square of indentations, you have two options: 1) If the indentations of this last set run horizontally, use only a portion of the tines to finish the column. 2) If the indentations of this last set run vertically, simply make them shorter.

- If there happens not to be the perfect amount of space remaining between the first and last columns on the side of the cake, then the final column may have to be a smidge wider or narrower than the rest. Don't worry: with so many alternating crosshatches, no one will notice the small discrepancy.

- If you make a square that is wobbly or in the wrong direction, you can easily repair it by gently smoothing away the mistake with a small offset spatula. The result does not have to be perfectly smooth, since you will be adding a heavy pattern over the repair.

Chapter 5
Borders and Inscriptions

Measuring, mixing, scraping and spreading have culminated in a sink full of dishes and a singularly splendid cake. All your elbow grease and determination deserve additional artistic effort. Whether you plan to lavish your cake with decorations or leave it relatively unadorned, the border and inscription will give it a crown of cakely glory.

Borders

A piped border adds both a decorative element and a clean finish to a cake. A border around the bottom of the cake creates a seamless transition between the presentation surface and the icing, covering any blemishes that may have cropped up as you transferred the cake to the presentation surface. Similarly, a border around the top of the cake can obscure icing that is not entirely even.

Smooth Scallop Border

Simplicity and versatility make the smooth scallop my preferred border. The smooth scallop is neither formal nor overly ornate, so it pairs well with any type of decoration. Smooth scallop borders are always piped using a round tip. The instructions on page 98 are for a border around the top of the cake. See the Bits & Nibbles (below) for the adjustments necessary for a bottom border. Before beginning, fit a pastry bag with a round tip and fill it with icing.

Bits & Nibbles

- To pipe a smooth scallop border around the bottom of the cake, hold the pastry bag horizontally, at a 45-degree angle to the side of the cake, at the Southeast (SE) position, with the tip hovering near the surface of the cake. Follow steps 2 to 4, shifting the angle of the bag toward you to create the indent in step 3.

- A smooth scallop border can be made with any size round tip, and a ridged scallop border (see Up Your Game, page 98) can be made with any size star tip. A good rule of thumb is to make sure the size of the tip is proportionate to the size of the cake. So if, for example, your cake is quite small, use a decorating tip with a smaller opening.

- To ensure that a top border remains perfectly round, allow the turntable to do its fair share of the work. After piping each scallop, rotate the turntable slightly so that you are always piping scallops directly in front of you.

Decorating Steps

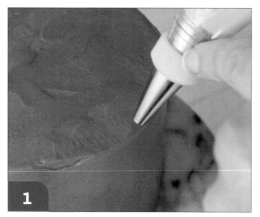

1

Hold the pastry bag at a 45-degree angle to the top of the cake, in the 3 o'clock direction, at the South (S) position. The tip should hover just above the surface.

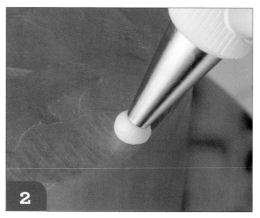

2

Squeeze the bag with moderate pressure so that the icing fans out and begins to make a rounded dollop.

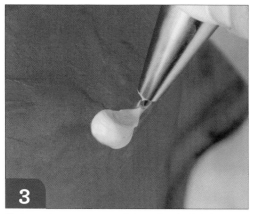

3

Reduce the pressure and drag the tip lightly through the dollop, shifting the bag to almost vertical to create an indent. Release the pressure completely while moving your hand forward to create a tapered point.

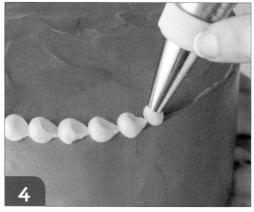

4

Spin the turntable slightly and make another scallop directly next to the first, on top of its tapered tail. Continue spinning and making scallops until you have a ring of scallops around the cake.

Up Your Game

If you are looking for a border that is a tad more classic and ornate, opt for the ridged scallop border. The technique is the same as for the smooth scallop, but it is executed with a star tip.

Dot Border

The advantage of the dot border is that it's straightforward and easy. There is also something innocent and happy about the dot border, a particular homespun attractiveness. The instructions below are for a border around the top of the cake. See the Bits & Nibbles on page 100 for the adjustments necessary for a bottom border. Before beginning, fit a pastry bag with a round tip and fill it with icing.

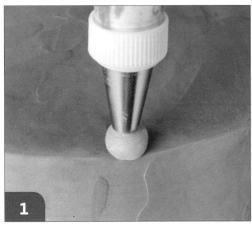

1

Hold the pastry bag vertically, at the South (S) position, with the tip hovering just above the cake. Squeeze the bag with moderate pressure until a fat dot forms and just begins to envelop the tip.

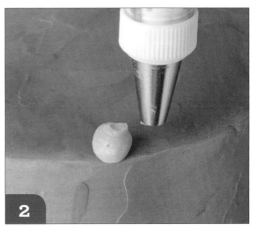

2

Completely release pressure on the bag before slowly moving it away to the side.

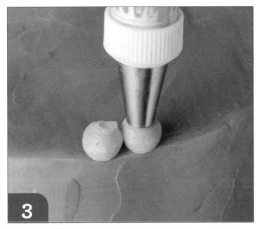

3

Spin the turntable slightly and make another dot directly next to the first.

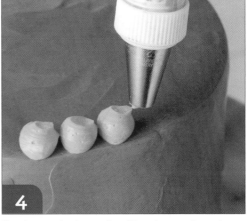

4

Continue spinning and making dots until you have a ring of dots around the cake.

Bits & Nibbles

- To pipe a dot border around the bottom of the cake, hold the pastry bag horizontally, at a 90-degree angle to the side of the cake, at the Southeast (SE) position, with the tip hovering near the surface of the cake. Continue to follow steps 1 to 4.

- A dot border can be made with any size round tip. The smaller the tip, the closer to the surface of the cake it should be held.

- A cake that has been decorated particularly sweetly, or for a child, looks terrific with large, fat dots in multiple colors.

- To ensure that a top border remains perfectly round, allow the turntable to do its fair share of the work. After piping each dot, rotate the turntable slightly so that you are always piping dots directly in front of you.

Up Your Game

Dot borders look particularly smashing in two or more colors.

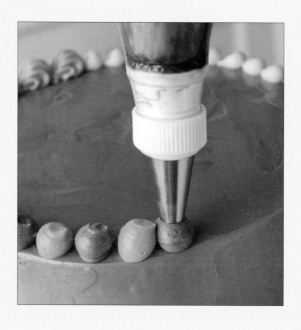

Inscriptions

You have a lifetime of practice writing, and your experience will serve you well, but writing on a cake is a tad different than writing on the page, and buttercream does not behave like ink. Practice will lead to improvement, but don't worry about the perfection of your inscription. With the majority of today's written communication executed on a keyboard, a handwritten message of any kind conveys an additional note of warmth and goodwill. Let the inscription reflect the personality of the decoration and your own individuality.

Sample Inscription Styles

1. All lowercase, simple print
2. All lowercase, simple print with serif added
3. All lowercase, simple print with dots added
4. All lowercase, fancy print in an arc
5. All uppercase, simple print with serif added
6. All lowercase, simple print made with dots using a star tip, with the letters in an arc
7. Uppercase and lowercase combination, fancy print
8. All uppercase, tall and thin simple print
9. All lowercase, short and squat simple print in an arc

There are endless styles in which to inscribe a cake. You can look online at different fonts for inspiration, and it's always fun to copy a fancy font, but your greatest success will come from inscribing cakes in a style you are already comfortable with: your everyday writing style. Here are some simple ways to trick out your usual handwriting:

- Write in all lowercase or all uppercase letters. If you want to distinguish a proper name or the start of a sentence, just make the first letter larger and/or taller, but maintain the lowercase and uppercase theme.

- Add serifs to each letter. A serif is a tiny line that is added to the top or bottom stroke of a letter. This technique can be used with uppercase or lowercase lettering.

- Add a dot to the top or bottom stroke of each letter. This technique is particularly appropriate for a child's cake and can be used with uppercase or lowercase lettering.

- Make each letter tall and thin, or stretch them out and make each letter short and squat.

- Make the first letter of each word, or the first and last letter of each word, particularly large and ornate.

- Write the inscription in a particular shape, such as an arc. If there is a decoration in the center of the cake, you could write the first half of the inscription in a rainbow-shaped arc on the top of the cake and the second half in a smile-shaped arc on the bottom, framing the decoration. Use a toothpick to lightly sketch out the shape before beginning to inscribe.

- Keep all the letters perfectly vertical or lean them all slightly forward or backward. Whatever slant you choose, keep it consistent.

- For a purposely jumbled, childlike look, stagger each letter, making one higher and the next one lower, and write them with different orientation, with some of the letters tilting to the right and some to the left.

- Create long, ornate, curling tails for the letters "g," "j," "p," "q" and "y."

- Alternate colors between each word or even between each letter.

- Emphasize a particular word by making it larger. It looks especially good when you make a name or a number larger. You can even switch to a bigger tip for extra emphasis.

Bits & Nibbles

- Inscriptions are most often piped using a round tip. The size of the tip used is dictated by the size of the cake and how much room you have to write the inscription.

- If writing a smooth and consistent inscription with a round tip is proving challenging, try switching to a star tip and creating letters by stringing small star-shaped dots together. An example of this technique can be seen in the orange "congratulations!" in the photo on page 101.

- Ease inscription jitters by first lightly writing the inscription with a toothpick. Make sure to leave a little bit more room in between each letter and word when using the toothpick, because the buttercream piping will be fatter than the impression the toothpick makes.

- Not happy with your inscription on the first go-round? Chill the cake in the fridge for 15 minutes, then pop off the inscription with a toothpick and try again.

Learn from My Mistakes

Looking at my sample inscription styles, you might have noticed that none of the inscriptions is in true cursive. The embarrassing truth is that I don't write in cursive — not in my everyday life and not on cakes. A cake decorator who doesn't write in cursive is an aberration, and for a long time I beat myself up about this. I love a gorgeous script, and for a while I tried writing inscriptions in cursive. My script improved, but I was never fully satisfied with the result. A lifetime of writing in print had made a lasting impact. Eventually I developed a style of printing that mimics writing in cursive (the green and turquoise inscription styles in the photo), but more important, I accepted that I wasn't going to be good at everything. I let myself off the hook and devoted myself to developing those skills that I knew I could do well and have fun doing.

Chapter 6
Embellishment

Decorating a cake doesn't necessarily mean creating elaborate piped decorations, or the tips, tools and cleanup associated with them. Embellishment can be as simple as adding color or texture, a spattering of sprinkles, candies or cookies, or an arrangement of flowers and fruit. An impressively decorated cake may be as close as your cupboard.

Satin Sashes

Like Maria from *The Sound of Music*, satin sashes of any color are among my favorite things. If, like me, you feel compelled to buy pretty ribbon for projects yet imagined, this cake is perfect for making fast work of random ribbon remnants.

Cake: 8-inch (20 cm) cake, iced in white with a Lath and Plaster finish (page 64) and chilled

Pastry Bags: 1 bag, fitted with a coupler

Tips: #4 round tip

Buttercream: ¼ cup (60 mL) white

Other Stuff: Squeeze bottle of corn syrup

28 inches (70 cm) medium-width black-and-white checked ribbon

60 inches (150 cm) thin black picot ribbon

30 inches (75 cm) wide black and white polka-dot grosgrain ribbon

Bag Prep: Fit the pastry bag with the round tip and fill it with white icing.

Cake Prep: Center the cake on the presentation surface, securing it with a dribble of corn syrup, and place it in the center of the turntable.

Up Your Game

Let your creativity and ribbon scraps run rampant. Layer, cross and stack ribbons in any pattern or combination you can imagine, and vary the position of the bow, even placing it on top of the cake.

Phraseology

There are dozens of different types of ribbons, but here are a couple used in this project:

- *Picot:* A thin, often satin ribbon with a series of small ornamental loops that form an edging. (Adapted from merriam-webster.com.)
- *Grosgrain:* A closely woven silk or rayon fabric with narrow horizontal ribbing. (From thefreedictionary.com.)

Decorating Steps

1 Affix the checked ribbon around the bottom of the cake (see New Trick, page 90).

2 Gently press one end of the picot ribbon to the cake, just above the overlap of the checked ribbon.

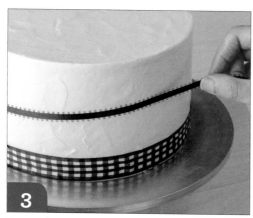

3 Wrap the picot ribbon around the cake so that it gradually climbs the side, nearing the top of the cake after one full rotation.

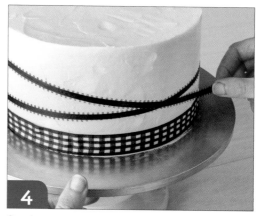

4 Continue to wrap the ribbon around the cake, but now gradually descend the side of the cake until it crosses itself and reaches the checked ribbon.

5 Use a small dab of icing to glue the end of the picot ribbon to the checked ribbon underneath so that it lies smooth.

6 Make a bow with the grosgrain ribbon. Use a generous squeeze of corn syrup to glue the bow to the checked ribbon border, near to but not covering the place where the picot ribbon crisscrosses.

Bits & Nibbles

- To avoid frayed ends that look like they were cut with your incisors, use very sharp scissors to cut the ribbons.

- This project works best with cakes that have nice straight vertical sides, which helps prevent the picot ribbon from puckering.

- Ribbon can soak up the oil from icing and become discolored. Navy blue and dark purple ribbon can skew toward black, and white or pale ribbon can become translucent. Keep this in mind when selecting ribbons for your cake.

- When wrapping the picot ribbon in steps 3 and 4, wrap tightly enough that the ribbon lies smooth and flat, but not so tight that it cuts into the icing. The ribbon will naturally adhere to the icing.

Meadow

There's nothing more scrumptious than cake or more inherently exquisite than fresh flowers, but Aristotle may have been referring to the combination when he said, "The whole is greater than the sum of its parts." Magic happens when flour meets flower.

Cake: 8-inch (20 cm) cake, iced in soft yellow with a Lath and Plaster finish (page 64) and chilled

Pastry Bags: 1 bag, fitted with a coupler

Tips: #6 round tip

Buttercream: ½ cup (125 mL) soft yellow

Other Stuff: Corn syrup
28 inches (70 cm) black-and-white checked ribbon
1 small sunflower
6 sprigs of purple statice
6 sprigs of yellow statice
6 sprigs of dianthus in shades of pink and purple
2 ornamental cabbage blossoms
5 stems of small golden zinnias, plus 3 or more buds

Bag Prep: Fit the pastry bag with the round tip and fill it with soft yellow icing.

Cake Prep: While the cake is chilling, soak, rinse and dry the flowers (see Bits & Nibbles, page 114) and group by type. Center the cake on the presentation surface, securing it with a dribble of corn syrup, and place it in the center of the turntable. Affix the ribbon around the bottom of the cake (see New Trick, page 90). Let the cake come to room temperature, then pipe a Smooth Scallop Border (see page 97) around the bottom of the cake, in front of the ribbon border.

Decorating Steps

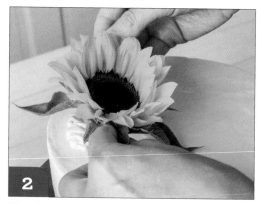

1

Pipe a small hill of icing on top of the cake, about 1 inch (2.5 cm) from the edge. (The hill helps give both stability and prominence to the sunflower.)

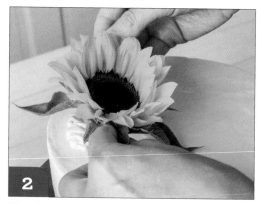

2

Trim the sunflower's stem very short, almost to the base. Place the sunflower on the icing hill, angling it toward the center of the cake.

3

Trim 2 statice stems to about 3 inches (7.5 cm). Place one on each side of the sunflower, creating a crescent on top of the cake. Leave enough room to add flowers between the statice and the sunflower.

4

Trim the stems of 2 dianthus sprigs and place 1 sprig on either side of the sunflower.

5

Pull 3 to 4 leaves off a cabbage blossom and place them so that they radiate out from the back of the sunflower.

6

Trim the stems of the zinnias to about 1 inch (2.5 cm) long. Arrange 2 zinnias on either side of the sunflower, one facing the center of the cake and one facing away. Place the last zinnia behind the sunflower.

7

Now that all the foundational flowers are in place, it's time to fill in the gaps with filler flowers, including dianthus buds and greens and groups of 2 or 3 zinnia buds.

8

Trim a few statice that have a natural bend to them and arrange them to cascade over the side of the cake.

9

Add leaves of any sort to fill out the bouquet, tucking them under flowers to reinforce the crescent shape and accent foundational flowers, or placing them vertically in between flowers for height and fullness.

10

Continue to add flowers and leaves until the crescent is distinct and bountiful.

Phraseology

- *Anchor Flower:* The focal point of the cake — the siren flower that naturally draws the eye. In this project, the sunflower is the anchor.

- *Foundational Flowers:* The flowers that create the outline or parameters of your arrangement.

- *Filler Flowers:* Flowers that fill in gaps in the arrangement after the anchor and foundational flowers have been placed. Filler flowers are often smaller in size and come in clusters. Sprigs of leaves and ornamental berries can also act as fillers.

Bits & Nibbles

- Some flowers are edible, but most are not. Popular edible flowers include clover, dandelions, roses, lavender, sunflowers, chamomile, pansies, nasturtiums, marigolds and tulips. Be aware that even when a flower or petal is edible, other portions of the plant may not be. And even edible flowers may not be fit for consumption if they have been treated with chemicals or pesticides. Purchase edible flowers from the produce department of your local grocery store or order them from a reputable vendor.

- Even if you don't plan on eating your arrangement, it's vital to thoroughly wash all flowers. Most flowers, including the ones used here, can be submerged in water. This will help ensure that no creepy crawlies escape onto your cake, and will also hydrate the flowers and extend their lives. Trim the stems and mix 2 tsp (10 mL) baking soda into a full sink of tepid (not cold) water. Gently agitate the blooms and soak them for about 30 minutes, allowing all the dirt and debris to sink to the bottom. Without stirring up the water, gently remove the flowers from the bath and give them a gentle rinse under the tap. Lay them in a single layer on kitchen or paper towels and pat dry. When the majority of water has dissipated, stand them in a vase of water.

- In this project, the flowers lie on the surface of the cake and are not inserted directly into it. Before serving this cake, I would scrape off any icing that came in contact with the flowers. But for added insurance that you are avoiding any possible contamination, trim disposable plastic straws to a length just longer than the flower stems. Insert the straws into the cake and the flowers into the straws.

- If you're concerned that your flowers will wilt before the celebration, you can purchase small plastic containers with water-tight lids that hold water and can be inserted directly into the cake.

- Pluck and set aside the leaves of all your flowers for use as filler in the arrangement. Mix and match blooms and leaves. You can use scissors to trim leaves into interesting shapes or more proportionate sizes.

- Have more flowers on hand than you anticipate using. You never know what might happen or how many gaps will need to be filled.

- Use icing as needed to glue flowers and leaves in place or to build small hills for lift.

Cinematic

This cake is ready for its close-up. It's every kid's dream: a double feature spotlighting both movie candy and cake, for twice the sweetness and twice the fun.

Cake: 8-inch (20 cm) cake, roughly iced (see Phraseology, page 61) in red

Pastry Bags: 1 bag, fitted with a coupler

Tips: #30 (or similar) star tip

Buttercream: ¾ cup (175 mL) red

Other Stuff: Corn syrup
Straight spatula
16-oz (500 g) bag of black licorice ropes
16-oz (500 g) bag of red licorice ropes
15 black nonpareil-covered gummy berries (approx.)
15 red nonpareil-covered gummy berries (approx.)

Bag Prep: Fit the pastry bag with the star tip and fill it with red icing.

Cake Prep: Center the cake on the presentation surface, securing it with a dribble of corn syrup, and place it in the center of the turntable.

Bits & Nibbles

- If you're unable to get your hands on nonpareil-covered gummy berries, shoot for vintage movie candy such as Dots or jujubes. But anything that's edible and that matches the cake will do.

- When you go to place your last rope in step 6, you may find that your last rope is the same color as your first. In this case, I like to split the difference. Cut one of each color rope in half and place the half-ropes tip to tip as the last rope in the ring.

- Though the rosettes on this cake are much smaller than the cupcake rosettes on page 239, the technique for making them is exactly the same.

Decorating Steps

1

Using a straight spatula, make a spiral on the top of the cake as described in steps 5 and 6 of Spiral (page 72).

2

Snip off the squashed flat end on one side of each licorice rope.

3

Hold one licorice rope at a slanting angle against the side of the cake to determine how long the ropes should be cut. Pinch the rope with your fingers to mark where to make the cut.

4

Cut the rope, then hold it against the cake to double-check that it is the correct length. Use this rope as a measuring stick and cut the remaining ropes to the same length. You can cut several ropes at once.

5

Keeping your measuring stick rope back in case you need to cut more ropes, begin to place the ropes at a slanting angle against the side of the cake, alternating between red and black.

6

Continue to place ropes until the cake is fully ringed with licorice ropes.

Using red icing, pipe small rosettes (see Rosette, page 239) snug up against each other around the perimeter on top of the cake. The rosettes should be larger than the base of a gummy berry.

Place a gummy berry in the center of each rosette, alternating between red and black.

Cream Puff

Though absent the eponymous cream puff, this cake delivers all the sugary fluff that the name evokes, along with a powerfully sweet visual wallop, thanks to the dazzling pastel array of macarons, meltaways and other dainties.

Cake: 8-inch (20 cm) cake, iced in pale yellow with a Polished finish (page 59)

Pastry Bags: 1 bag, fitted with a coupler

Tips: #6 round tip

Buttercream: ¼ cup (60 mL) soft purple

Other Stuff: Corn syrup
1 mini Belgian waffle
Soft purple Candy Glaze (see New Trick, page 122)
Parchment paper
Straight spatula
7 pastel macarons
A handful of pastel mint nonpareil kisses
5 large marshmallows
Toothpicks
A handful of soft green mint malt balls
A handful of pastel meltaway mint candies

Bag Prep: Fit the pastry bag with the round tip and fill it with soft purple icing.

Cake Prep: Center the cake on the presentation surface, securing it with a dribble of corn syrup, and place it in the center of the turntable. Dip the Belgian waffle in the Candy Glaze and let it dry completely on parchment paper. Meanwhile, partially glaze the cake with the remaining Candy Glaze (see New Trick, page 123).

New Trick: Candy Glaze

Glaze can be used to coat a cake with glossy goodness that needs no further decoration or to partially coat a cake for added texture and dimension (as in the New Trick below). Or it can be drizzled over a simple Bundt cake for added ooey-gooey flavor. This recipe makes about $2\frac{1}{4}$ cups (550 mL) glaze.

1. Place 12 oz (375 g) colored or white candy coating wafers in the top of a double boiler over 2 inches (5 cm) of water. Gently heat the water on low heat until it begins to steam.
2. Stir the candy melts constantly until they are melted and smooth.
3. Stir in $\frac{1}{3}$ cup (75 mL) heavy or whipping (35%) cream, then stir in small quantities of food coloring as necessary until you have reached your desired color. At this point, the glaze should be completely smooth but not hot, and should have a viscosity similar to that of honey.

Bits & Nibbles

- If you don't want to bother with a double boiler, you can quickly melt the candy coating wafers in the microwave, heating them in 10-second intervals and stirring between each interval to avoid scorching.

- Why use candy coating wafers and not white chocolate for the glaze? White chocolate is finicky, and it's difficult to achieve a smooth, even finish with a white chocolate glaze. Candy coating wafers were created for just such a purpose and will make your decorating experience that much easier and more predictable.

- Candy coating wafers come in a handful of fun colors. You can save yourself some hassle by purchasing colored candy wafers instead of adding food coloring to melted white candy wafers.

Phraseology

Double Boiler: A double boiler is essentially two pots, one of which fits partway inside the other. Water is heated, simmered or boiled in the lower pot to cook, warm or melt food in the upper pot without scorching. A double boiler is commonly used to make custards, curds and, of course, Swiss buttercream icing. If you don't have a double boiler, you can use a heatproof mixing bowl placed over a saucepan.

New Trick: Partially Glazing a Cake

When glazing a cake, ensure that the glaze is smooth and easily poured, *but not hot*. Lukewarm glaze will nicely coat a cake without melting the icing and harming your finish.

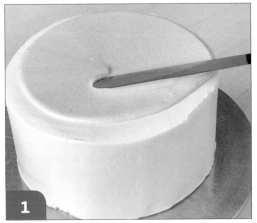

1

Pour the glaze into the center of the cake. While rotating the turntable, use the straight spatula to spread the glaze evenly from the center to the edges.

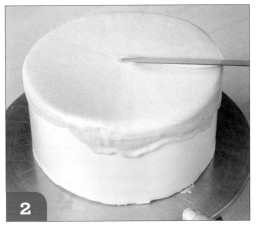

2

When the glaze is evenly distributed across the top and is nearing the edges of the cake, make a measured final rotation or two to push the glaze over the edge until it begins to drip down the side.

Learn from My Mistakes

Glazing a cake can take a little getting used to. If you happen to overpour and have dribbles that reach all the way down the side of the cake, wait until the glaze hardens, then remove the rigid puddle. Any flaws in the glaze can be concealed with candies and such.

Piece of Cake

If glazing a cake is a bit too finicky for your liking, then nix the glaze and just pile the delicacies on top of the naked icing.

Decorating Steps

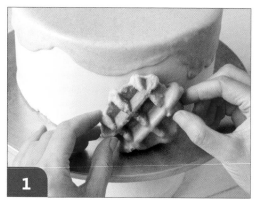

1

Place the dipped Belgian waffle on end on the presentation surface, leaning it against the side of the cake so that it is nearly vertical. (The icing is soft and will work as glue to hold the waffle in place.)

2

Place a macaron on an angle next to the waffle, using both the side of the cake and a nonpareil kiss as support.

3

Pipe a large dollop of icing onto the back of a nonpareil kiss and place it on the presentation surface at a different angle to the side of the cake.

4

Place a macaron at an angle against the nonpareil, securing it with icing if necessary.

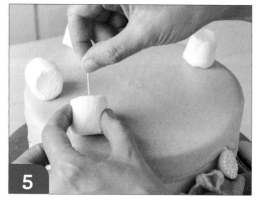

5

Use icing to glue 5 marshmallows, evenly separated, on top of the cake, around the perimeter. Use toothpicks to secure a couple of them at interesting angles.

6

Using icing as glue, lean a macaron against each marshmallow, changing the angle of lean with each macaron.

7

Fill in the remaining space around the perimeter with nonpareil kisses, malt balls and meltaway mint candies.

8

Take a few steps away from the cake for perspective. Add candy as needed to create balance and harmony around the perimeter and on the side of the cake.

Up Your Game

Use icing glue and toothpicks to dangle candy precariously over the edge of the cake or to create a waterfall of candies over the side.

For a completely different look, cover the cake in chocolate glaze and top it with vintage candies in a bright palette.

Animal Crackers

Chubby baby elephants and pastel nonpareils kick up the cute factor without stumbling into the territory of children's cakes so pink and saccharine as to spontaneously pop the fillings from your teeth. As adorable as the elephants on this cake may be, don't make them the only animals in your cracker box. Let this project inspire creative use of neglected cookie cutters from times long past.

Cake: 8-inch (20 cm) cake, iced in soft blue with a Spiral finish (page 71)

Pastry Bags: 1 bag, fitted with a coupler

Tips: #8 round tip

Buttercream: ½ cup (125 mL) soft blue
1 cup (250 mL) pale pink

Other Stuff: Corn syrup
Small offset spatula
Parchment paper
Pastel nonpareils
Cutting board
Medium-size elephant cookie cutter
¼ cup (60 mL) cornstarch on a small plate
Eraser-tipped pencil

Bag Prep: Fit the pastry bag with the round tip and fill it with soft blue icing.

Cake Prep: Center the cake on the presentation surface, securing it with a dribble of corn syrup, and place it in the center of the turntable.

Decorating Steps

1

Use the small offset spatula to scoop the pale pink icing onto a piece of parchment paper and smooth it out into an even layer about $\frac{1}{4}$ inch (5 mm) thick.

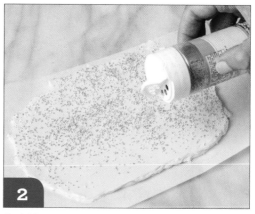

2

Sprinkle an even coating of pastel nonpareils over the pink icing.

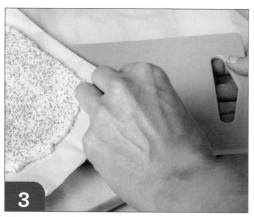

3

Slide the parchment paper onto the cutting board and refrigerate for 20 to 30 minutes or until the icing is thoroughly chilled.

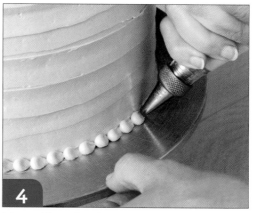

4

Meanwhile, using the soft blue icing, pipe a Smooth Scallop Border (see page 97) around the bottom of the cake.

5

Prepare a second piece of parchment paper to receive the elephant cutouts. Remove the pink icing from the fridge and, working quickly, dip the cookie cutter, cutter side down, in the cornstarch.

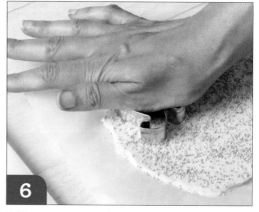

6

With even pressure from your palm, press the cookie cutter down into the pink icing until it passes all the way through.

7

Lift the cookie cutter, with the elephant still inside. Hover the cutter just above the new piece of parchment and use the pad of your finger and the eraser end of the pencil to gently tap the elephant out.

8

Cleaning the cutter and dipping it in cornstarch between each cut, repeat steps 6 and 7 to make at least two more elephants. Slide the parchment onto the cutting board and refrigerate until completely chilled, about 15 minutes.

9

Working quickly with cool hands, pick up the first elephant and press it onto the side of the cake, near the bottom, with the front feet slightly higher than the back feet (so the elephant appears to be traveling upward).

10

Press the other two elephants against the side of the cake in an upward diagonal from the first. It is okay if the final elephant reaches above the top edge of the cake.

Learn from My Mistakes

I became enamored with this elephant cookie cutter as soon as I saw it. What I didn't take into account was its narrow trunk, or more specifically, how challenging it would be to remove the narrow icing trunk from the cookie cutter. Full confession: I lost quite a few trunks. If you don't want the hassle of possible "truncation," choose cutters that are not exceedingly ornate and that do not have overly narrow openings.

Bits & Nibbles

- Parchment paper can be a tad temperamental when you're attempting to spread an even layer of icing over it. If desired, you can use easily removable tape to attach the paper either to the counter or directly onto the cutting board before you start.

- Since an eraser-tipped pencil is a lot thinner than a fingertip, it is used here to help us tap the narrow trunk of the elephant out of the cookie cutter. If you're worried about the eraser not being sanitary, remove any dark areas by rubbing it on a blank piece of paper, then wash the eraser with dish detergent.

- Buttercream cutouts can be squirrelly, and it takes practice to tap them from the cookie cutter without accidental amputation of icing limbs. Be sure to make more cutouts than are required so that you have enough remaining even if a few get dismembered.

- Use a damp kitchen towel or paper towel to clean icing off the cookie cutter between each cut.

- In steps 9 and 10, give each elephant a good press with the pad of your finger to ensure that it is well affixed to the side of the cake.

- Like Dumbo, these elephants defy gravity, and although the cutouts are sturdier than you might imagine, I would not recommend preparing this cake if you need to travel any farther than between your kitchen and dining room.

Up Your Game

If you end up with more intact elephants than the directions call for, you can create an elephant train that climbs the entire circumference of the cake, or you can lay a couple of elephants flat on top of the cake.

Converse Confetti

Nothing says happy like sprinkles. Donuts, ice cream and cake are elevated from mundane snack to edible celebration with a quick dip in the rainbow sprinkle jackpot. If you worry that sprinkles are intended exclusively for the tykes (they're not), then add a little badass black sugar to your mixture.

Project 1: Positive Space

Cake: 8-inch (20 cm) cake, iced in watermelon red with a Polished finish (page 59)

Other Stuff: ¼ cup (60 mL) multicolored confetti
¼ cup (60 mL) multicolored pastel confetti
¼ cup (60 mL) multicolored jimmies
¼ cup (60 mL) multicolored nonpareils
¼ cup (60 mL) silver dragées
¼ cup (60 mL) black sugar crystals
Corn syrup
Cookie cutters (I used a "1" and a "6")
Eraser-tipped pencil
Tweezers or toothpick

Phraseology

- *Confetti:* Flat disk-shaped bits of candy for decorating candy, cakes and cookies.
- *Jimmies:* Rod-shaped bits of candy used as a topping for ice cream, cakes and other sweets. (Adapted from the Dictionary of American Regional English.)
- *Nonpareils:* Tiny, smooth pellets of colored sugar for decorating candy, cakes and cookies. (Adapted from Dictionary.com.)
- *Dragées:* Small beadlike pieces of candy, usually silver-colored, used to decorate cookies and cakes. (Adapted from Dictionary.com.)

Decorating Steps

1

Mix the 6 types of sprinkles together in a bowl that is the same diameter or larger than the diameter of the cake.

2

Taking great care, balance the cake on your dominant hand, holding it over the bowl of sprinkles. With your free hand, palm a handful of the sprinkle mix and press it onto the bottom edge of the cake.

3

Continue to press handfuls of sprinkles around the bottom edge of the cake, rotating it as necessary, until a full border is created.

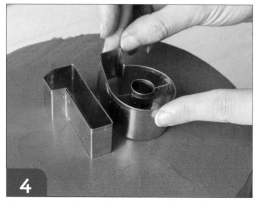

4

Center the cake on the presentation surface, securing it with a dribble of corn syrup, and place it in the center of the turntable. Gently place the cookie cutters on top of the cake, ensuring that they are centered.

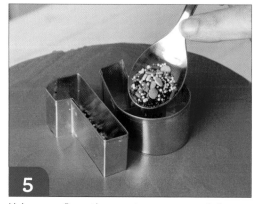

5

Using your fingertips or a teaspoon, carefully scatter or pour an even layer of the sprinkle mix into the cookie cutters.

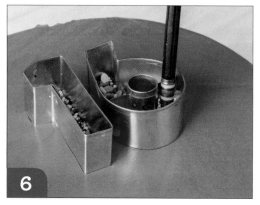

6

Use the eraser end of the pencil to gently and evenly distribute the sprinkles into the corners and crevices of the cookie cutters.

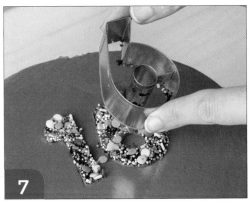

Using both hands, gently pull the cookie cutters straight up, leaving the sprinkled imprints behind.

Use the tweezers or a toothpick to remove any stray sprinkles that detract from the crisp image left by the cookie cutters.

Project 2: Negative Space

Cake: 6-inch (15 cm) cake, iced in white with a Polished finish (page 59)

Other Stuff: Cookie cutters (I used a "4" and a "0")
Parchment paper
Scissors
⅓ cup (75 mL) multicolored confetti
⅓ cup (75 mL) multicolored pastel confetti
⅓ cup (75 mL) multicolored jimmies
⅓ cup (75 mL) multicolored nonpareils
⅓ cup (75 mL) silver dragées
⅓ cup (75 mL) black sugar crystals
Corn syrup
Eraser-tipped pencil
Tweezers or toothpick

Project Prep: Place the cookie cutters on top of a piece of parchment paper and trace their outlines. Cut out the outlines and set aside.

Mix the 6 types of sprinkles together in a bowl that is the same diameter or larger than the diameter of the cake.

Taking great care, balance the cake on your dominant hand, holding it over the bowl of sprinkles. With your free hand, palm a handful of the sprinkle mix and press it onto the side of the cake.

3

Continue to press handfuls of sprinkles onto the sides of the cake, rotating it as necessary, until they are completely covered with sprinkles.

4

Center the cake on the presentation surface, securing it with a dribble of corn syrup, and place it in the center of the turntable. Gently place the cookie cutters on top of the cake, ensuring that they are centered.

5

Using your fingertip, without using too much pressure, rub a bit of icing around the top edge of each cookie cutter, to act as glue. Gently press the matching parchment template onto each cookie cutter.

6

Scatter the sprinkle mix in a thin, even coating over the top of the cake until the entire top is coated. Press the sprinkles gently into the icing, taking special care around the outside of the cookie cutters.

7

Remove the parchment templates from the cookie cutters. Using your fingertips, carefully drop sprinkle mix into any cutouts in the cookie cutters.

8

Use the eraser end of the pencil to gently and evenly distribute the sprinkles into the corners and crevices in the cutouts of the cookie cutters.

Using both hands, gently pull the cookie cutters straight up, leaving the sprinkled imprints behind.

Use the tweezers or a toothpick to remove any stray sprinkles that detract from the crisp image left by the cookie cutters.

Bits & Nibbles

- I used saturated colors and number-shaped cookie cutters to decorate these cakes, but you can use any colors and types of sprinkle and any combination of cutters, placed in any pattern. Whatever combination of sprinkles you use, choose some small nonpareils or colored sugar to ensure that all the corners and crevices can be tightly filled, resulting in a crisp, distinct image.

- Using sprinkles this way can be a mess-producing affair. To keep the kitchen tidy, place a baking sheet under the sprinkle bowl and another one under the turntable to catch stray sprinkles.

- When pouring sprinkles into the bowl, pour them near the bottom. Sprinkles have a surprising ability to bounce and roll right out of containers.

- Since an eraser-tipped pencil is a lot thinner than a fingertip, it is used in these projects to help distribute the sprinkles into small areas within the cookie cutters. If you're worried about the eraser not being sanitary, remove any dark areas by rubbing it on a blank piece of paper, then wash the eraser with dish detergent.

- If you don't own a funnel and you want to pour leftovers of your sprinkle mix into a narrow container, fold a generous sheet of parchment paper in half, creating a sharp crease. Gently pour the sprinkle mix into the center of the parchment. Lift the parchment, closing off one end and bunching it in your hand. Rest the pointed crease of the non-bunched end inside the edge of the container and gently funnel the sprinkles in.

Dusted

Here, an old-school decorating technique — stenciling with sugar — enjoys an unapologetically hip renaissance with the unexpected use of cocoa powder and a contemporary pattern.

Cake: 6-inch (15 cm) cake, iced in light blue with a Lath and Plaster finish (page 64) and chilled

Pastry Bags: 1 bag, fitted with a coupler

Tips: #4 round tip (or any similar size)

Buttercream: ¼ cup (60 mL) light blue

Other Stuff: Corn syrup
28 inches (70 cm) wide burlap ribbon
Chevron stencil
½ cup (125 mL) unsweetened cocoa powder
Fine-mesh sieve

Bag Prep: Fit the pastry bag with the round tip and fill it with light blue icing.

Cake Prep: Center the cake on the presentation surface, securing it with a dribble of corn syrup, and place it in the center of the turntable.

Cake Debate

Q: Dear Carey, To my delight, I successfully dusted the dickens out of my cake, but overnight my delicate dusting took on the appearance of an expanding patchy fungus. Please explain.

Sincerely, Deteriorating Dust

A: Dear DD, You have a talent for creepy analogies, but you do not have a creeping cake fungus. The patchy appearance is caused by the absorption of oil from the icing into your cocoa or sugar. There's no remedy for this condition, so accept it as a natural contribution to the inherent beauty of a handcrafted cake. One person's fungus is another's confectionary masterpiece.

Decorating Steps

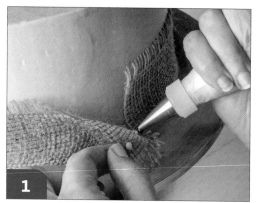

1

Affix the ribbon around the bottom of the cake (see New Trick, page 90).

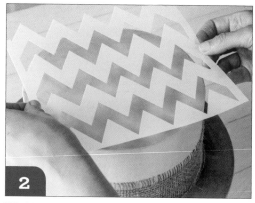

2

Working quickly so that the icing remains chilled, hover the chevron stencil over the surface of the cake until it is nicely centered, then gently rest it on the surface.

3

Place the cocoa powder in the sieve. Tap the sieve against your finger, creating a fine dust that settles over the top of the cake. Continue to dust a fine, even layer of cocoa over the cake until no blue shows through.

4

Using both hands, slowly and gently lift the stencil off of the cake, ensuring that the cocoa does not spill.

Learn from My Mistakes

To avoid an unexpected kitchen blizzard, make sure to turn off all fans and air vents — they can send light-as-air cocoa powder and sugar flying.

Bits & Nibbles

- It goes without saying that you can use any stencil for this project. Take a stroll through your local arts and crafts store for inspiration. If you're looking for something specific, try searching online.

- Dusting a stencil on the side of a cake would require bending the law of gravity, so instead make generous use of ribbon. Stack, layer and cross ribbons to suit your fancy and cake design.

Up Your Game

For a more complex design, use multiple colors of powdered (icing) sugar in place of the cocoa. Making powdered sugar pop with color is as easy as mixing luster dust or powdered food coloring into the sugar until your desired color is achieved.

If you're keen on replicating a specific image, you can make your own stencil with the help of a photocopier and a utility knife. I took full advantage of this when I became hoof-over-horns smitten with a black-and-white photo of a deer and just had to create a cake-top decoration with it.

Interpunct

Before there were spaces between words, there was the interpunct, a small centered dot used for between-word separation, a floating period, if you will, a signal to take a breath. If my musical abilities extended beyond a stuttering rendition of Beethoven's "Für Elise," I would christen my band Interpunct. Being that my gig is cake, "interpunct" is a stellar descriptor for this sweet project: dots galore, all small and centered.

Cake: 6-inch (15 cm) cake, iced in medium soft green with a Polished finish (page 59)

Pastry Bags: 2 bags, fitted with couplers

Tips: #8 round tip
#2 round tip

Buttercream: ½ cup (125 mL) medium soft green
½ cup (125 mL) pale soft green

Other Stuff: Corn syrup

Bag Prep: Fit one pastry bag with the #8 tip and fill it with medium soft green icing. Fit the other bag with the #2 tip and fill it with pale soft green icing.

Cake Prep: Center the cake on the presentation surface, securing it with a dribble of corn syrup, and place it in the center of the turntable.

Piece of Cake

Like the look, but can't be bothered with scads of microscopic dots? This design is easily simplified by using a #4 round tip instead of the miniscule #2 and omitting the majority of the dots. Pipe vertical lines of 3 dots interspersed with lines of 2 dots.

New Trick: Piping a Dot

1. Fit a pastry bag with a small round tip and fill it with icing. Hover the tip just above the cake (if piping the dot on top) or in front of the cake (if piping the dot on the side) and squeeze the bag with moderate pressure until a small dot forms and just begins to envelop the tip.

2. Completely release pressure on the bag before slowly moving it away to the side.

Bits & Nibbles

- Are your eyes crossing and your vision becoming blurry from dotting? Good! This dot disorientation allows you to shift visual perspective. Squint your eyes and release yourself from the vertical alignment of the dots. You'll begin to see the lines as diagonal, which allows for an alternative method of dot alignment.

- While piping the last row of dots, you might notice that it does not line up with the first. Forget about it! The dots are so small and numerous, not a soul will notice. And remember, a cake can only be viewed from one side, so a strategic rotation can easily hide any misalignment.

- If you're overcome with a fit of nerves, or decorating in extreme cold, then you may want to save this project for another day. An overly shaky hand can cause you to unintentionally dig the decorating tip into the icing or bump your beautifully formed dots.

Cake Debate

Q: Dear Carey, These tiny dots are worse than the hives I got when I ate shellfish at Coney Island last summer. Not for the life of me can I whip these disobedient dots into straight lines.

Thank You, One Dot Over the Deep End

A: Dear ODOTDE, If you're comparing sugar-laced icing to an allergic reaction, you're doing something wrong, and I know what it is: you're being too hard on yourself. Stop it right now and accept your straying dots for the wonderfully delicious disasters they may be. If you think I have a special talent for dot discipline, you are mistaken. My lines are crooked too, and guess what? With all these dozens of dots, no one will notice.

Decorating Steps

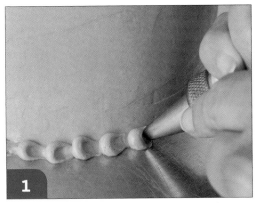

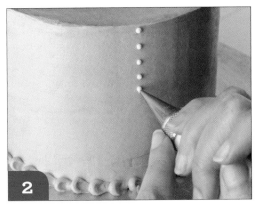

1

Using the medium soft green icing, pipe a Smooth Scallop Border (see page 97) around the bottom of the cake.

2

Using the pale soft green icing, pipe a vertical line of tiny dots from the top of the cake to the bottom.

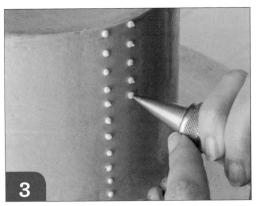

3

Pipe an identical vertical line of dots about 1 inch (2.5 cm) from the first, ensuring that the dots align horizontally.

4

Pipe a third line of dots in between the first two, staggering these dots so that each is centered vertically between two dots on either side.

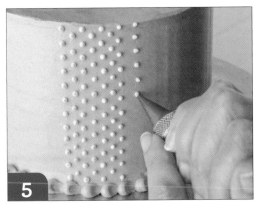

5

Continue piping lines as in steps 3 and 4 until the last line of dots meets the first.

Up Your Game

Do you have a slightly obsessive-compulsive component to your personality? You can smooth the tip of each dot by dipping your finger in a cup of water and gently tapping the pointed top. Be forewarned: these diminutive dots can be pancaked flat in an instant with a tad too much pressure.

Santa Fe

Shifting desert colors and strong geometric patterns bring the spirit of woven textiles from the arid southwestern U.S. to this cake. Dots, frequently so plump and sweet when used in cake decorating, have buckled on their spurs and six-shooters and rustled up a serious statement cake.

Cake: 6-inch (15 cm) cake, iced in green-yellow with a Polished finish (page 59) and chilled

Pastry Bags: 4 pastry bags, fitted with couplers

Tips: Four #3 round tips

Buttercream: ½ cup (125 mL) salmon
½ cup (125 mL) soft pink
½ cup (125 mL) turquoise
½ cup (125 mL) sky blue

Other Stuff: Corn syrup
28 inches (70 cm) white or pale green grosgrain ribbon

Bag Prep: Fit each pastry bag with a round tip and fill it with one of the four icing colors.

Cake Prep: Center the cake on the presentation surface, securing it with a dribble of corn syrup, and place it in the center of the turntable.

Decorating Steps

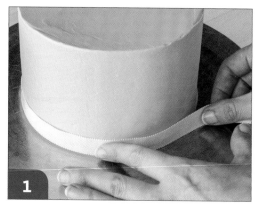

Affix the ribbon around the bottom of the cake (see New Trick, page 90), securing it with a little dab of green-yellow icing left over from icing the cake. Let the cake come to room temperature before starting step 2.

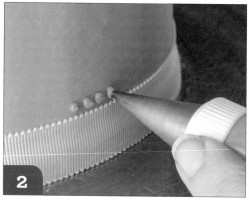

Using the salmon icing, pipe a neat row of 4 side-by-side dots just above the ribbon border to form the base of a pyramid.

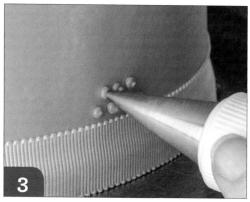

Pipe a line of 3 salmon dots centered directly above the first line.

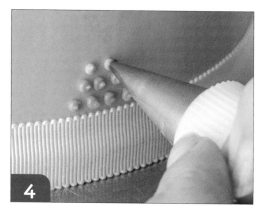

Using the soft pink icing, pipe 2 dots centered above the previous 3 dots.

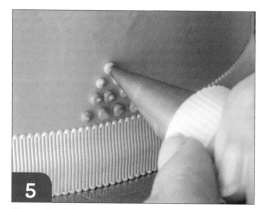

Pipe a final pink dot to complete the pyramid.

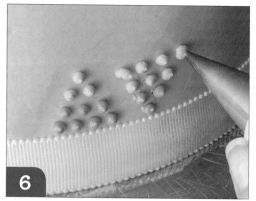

Pipe an upside-down pyramid next to the first pyramid, starting above the ribbon with 1 salmon dot, then 2 salmon dots, then 3 pink dots, then 4 pink dots.

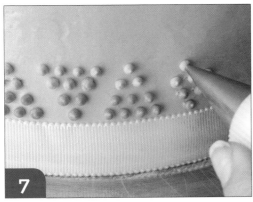

7 Continue to pipe pyramids, alternating between upright and upside-down pyramids, all the way around the cake.

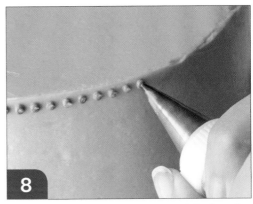

8 Using the turquoise icing, pipe a straight line of evenly spaced dots around the cake near the top.

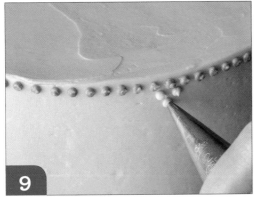

9 Using the sky blue icing, pipe 2 dots just below the line of turquoise dots, centering each sky blue dot between 2 turquoise dots. Place a final sky blue dot below and centered between the first 2.

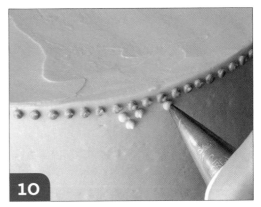

10 Center a single sky blue dot between the next 2 turquoise dots. Alternate between piping a 3-dot pyramid and piping a single dot all the way around the cake.

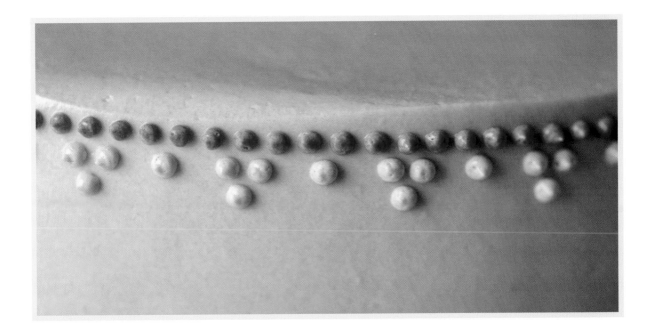

Bits & Nibbles

- See the New Trick on page 146 for details on how to make dots.

- The easiest way to line up dots is not necessarily the most intuitive. It's natural to pipe dots from left to right, like writing in English, but instead try piping the middle dot first. If there is a line of 4 dots and you need to pipe a row of 3 above it, start with the middle dot, centering it cozily above the middle 2 dots in the line below. Follow up by piping a dot on each side of the first.

- Every pyramid, whether upright or upside-down, should be the same height and width and should have salmon dots closest to the ribbon border and pink dots on top.

- Make sure to leave some space between each pyramid, so that your border does not end up looking like continuous horizontal lines of dots.

- The likelihood is slim that your last pyramid will line up perfectly with the first, and with the perfect amount of space between them. As you circle the cake and approach the point where you began, assess the situation to determine whether you should add more space between the last few pyramids to evenly divide the remaining space, making a clean finish.

- The top edge of your cake may not be straight and even, but the line of turquoise dots should be. A bit of green-yellow icing poking up will be much less noticeable than a snaking line of bright turquoise dots.

- Piping dots that are slightly askew or in the wrong color is par for the course when you're making this cake. Carefully lift off any erroneous dots with a toothpick or wooden skewer.

- If you use white ribbon, keep in mind that the ribbon may soak up oil from the icing and become translucent, taking on the color of the icing underneath.

French Kiss

If you listen to the glutinous siren call of this cake, you'll be hankering to flick a chubby dot straight into your chops. These dots are so plump and juicy, they'll remind you of an epic smooch. Simple sweetness and fat decadence combine to make for one irresistible cake.

Cake: 8-inch (20 cm) cake, iced in white with a Combed finish (page 77) or a Polished finish (page 59) and chilled

Pastry Bags: 5 bags, fitted with couplers

Buttercream: 1 cup (250 mL) pastel yellow
1 cup (250 mL) pastel orange
1 cup (250 mL) pastel red
1 cup (250 mL) pastel blue
1 cup (250 mL) pastel green

Other Stuff: Corn syrup
28 inches (70 cm) of coordinating ribbon
Straight spatula

Bag Prep: Fill each pastry bag with one of the five icing colors.

Cake Prep: Center the cake on the presentation surface, securing it with a dribble of corn syrup, and place it in the center of the turntable.

Piece of Cake

Not in the mood for a spiral top? Leave it smooth, or comb it to match the sides.

Cake Debate

Q: Dear Carey, These dots aren't just slightly misaligned, they've decided to congregate in mean-girl cliques at the bottom of the cake. I swear, I just turned my back for a second and the dots slid down the cake. Please help!

The Backsliding Baker

A: Dear TBB, If I had the opportunity to read your cake-encrusted palm, I'm sure I'd learn that you live in a warm and humid climate and that you chose to ice the cake with a Polished finish instead of a Combed finish. In a humid climate, you need to comb a little texture onto the cake to prevent the dots from sliding — and dragging you down with them.

New Trick: Coupler Dot

These giant dots are called coupler dots because the coupler is used on its own, with no tip attached. It's important to use a coupler and not just a bag with the tip cut off. The perfectly round opening of the coupler allows the icing to form a nicely rounded dot.

1. Fit a pastry bag with a coupler and fill it with icing. Hold the bag perpendicular to the cake, 1/8 to 1/4 inch (3 to 5 mm) from the surface.

2. Squeeze the bag with moderate pressure, keeping the bag stationary and allowing the icing to balloon out beyond the circumference of the coupler.

3. Stop squeezing. This seems obvious, but if you squeeze while pulling the bag away, you will create a bulbous icing cone instead of a perky tipped dot.

4. Gently pull the bag away from the cake.

Bits & Nibbles

- If you live in a warm, humid climate, be sure to use a Combed finish rather than a Polished finish, to prevent the dots from sliding down the sides of the cake.

- For smooth, bubble-free dots, give your icing a good beating or stir before starting.

- If your dots are splitting, you are making them overly large. Find that sweet spot where your dot is plump and luscious but not split. Practice on the surface of the turntable before decorating the cake. (The technique is the same on a horizontal surface as on a vertical one.)

- Make identical twin mini cupcakes to accompany your French Kiss cake by piping a coupler-sized dot on top of each.

Decorating Steps

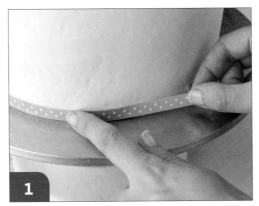

1

Affix the ribbon around the bottom of the cake (see New Trick, page 90). Let the cake come to room temperature before starting step 2.

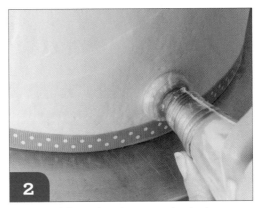

2

Using any icing color, pipe a coupler dot just above the ribbon border.

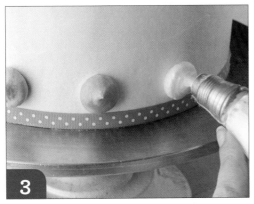

3

Rotating through the icing colors, continue to pipe coupler dots around the base of the cake, with equal space between each dot.

4

Starting with a different color than the one used to start the bottom row of dots, pipe a row of dots around the cake near the top, aligning each dot vertically with one below it.

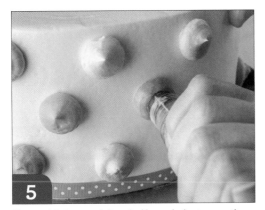

5

Pipe a third row of dots halfway in between the top and bottom rows, staggering each dot so that it is centered horizontally between 2 dots above and below it.

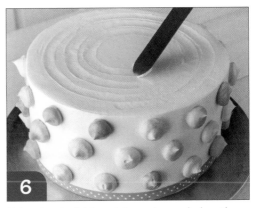

6

Using the straight spatula, make a spiral on the top of the cake, starting from the outside and working toward the middle. (For more details, follow steps 5 and 6 of Spiral, page 72.)

Stars and Stripes

Cakes awash with tiny starfish and buttercream stripes reminiscent of retro candy sticks add up to a forkful of nostalgia and summer days on the shore. But switch the colors to shades of pale blue, and your cake decorations are transformed into snowflakes and icicles. Let these simple, straightforward cakes be the answer to the dessert question for your seasonal celebrations.

Project 1: Stars

Cake: 6-inch (15 cm) cake, roughly iced (see Phraseology, page 61) in any shade of orange

Pastry Bags: 4 bags, fitted with couplers

Tips: Four #15 star tips (or any star tips that fit on a standard coupler)

Buttercream: ½ cup (125 mL) pale orange
½ cup (125 mL) light orange
½ cup (125 mL) medium orange
½ cup (125 mL) dark orange

Other Stuff: Corn syrup

Bag Prep: Fit each pastry bag with a star tip and fill it with one of the four icing colors.

Cake Prep: Center the cake on the presentation surface, securing it with a dribble of corn syrup, and place it in the center of the turntable.

New Trick: Buttercream Stars

Creating a buttercream star is much the same as creating a buttercream dot. Learn one and you've wrangled them both.

1. Fit a pastry bag with a star tip and fill it with icing. Hover the tip just above the cake (if piping the star on top) or in front of the cake (if piping the star on the side) and squeeze the bag with moderate pressure until a small fat star with distinct ridges forms and just begins to envelop the tip.

2. Completely release pressure on the bag before slowly moving it away to the side. (Releasing pressure before moving the bag will ensure that your stars are relatively flat and do not resemble Hershey Kisses.)

Decorating Steps

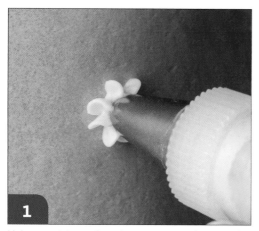

Using any icing color, pipe a star anywhere on the side of the cake.

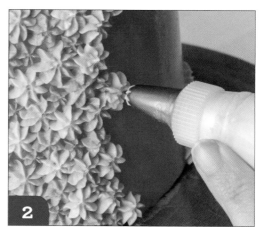

Rotating through the icing colors, continue to pipe stars, snug up against one another, until the entire cake is completely covered. There is no pattern; star placement is completely random.

Cake Debate

Q: Dear Carey, You said these cakes were simple and straightforward. I'm currently working on the Star cake, and my fatigued and cramping hand begs to differ.

Respectfully, Bamboozled

A: Dear Bamboozled, I feel this may require some clarification. These cakes are simple and straightforward, but they are not quick. One buttercream star is a cinch, but a few hundred can be tedious. I say pour a glass of wine, turn up the volume on an audiobook and be one with the cosmology of buttercream stars, because this cake is worth the effort.

Bits & Nibbles

- Don't have 4 star tips? In theory, you could use just 1 tip and switch it among the bags, but I would vigorously advise against it. Beg, borrow or steal to come up with 4 star tips, and you'll avoid added work and excess tedium.

- Occasionally take a step back when piping the stars to get a better view of your progress and determine if the 4 shades of orange are evenly distributed.

- When piping stripes, speed and pressure will determine if the ridges are straight as a pin or ruffled. But it matters little either way: ruffles add interest and texture to the cake.

Project 2: Stripes

Cake: 8-inch (20 cm) cake, iced in dark orange with a Polished finish (page 59) or a Lath and Plaster finish (page 64)

Pastry Bags: 4 bags, fitted with couplers

Tips: Four #32 star tips (or any star tips of similar size that fit on a standard coupler; avoid tiny star tips)

Other Stuff: Corn syrup

Buttercream: 1 cup (250 mL) pale orange
1 cup (250 mL) light orange
1 cup (250 mL) medium orange
1 cup (250 mL) dark orange

Bag Prep: Fit each pastry bag with a star tip and fill it with one of the four icing colors.

Cake Prep: Center the cake on the presentation surface, securing it with a dribble of corn syrup, and place it in the center of the turntable.

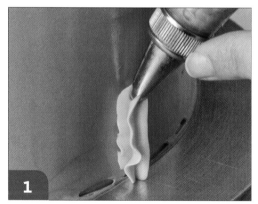

Choose any icing color and hold the pastry bag at the base of the cake at the south (S) position. Tilt the bag up to a 45-degree angle. With firm pressure, simultaneously squeeze the bag and run your hand vertically up the side of the cake. Release pressure at the top.

Rotating through the icing colors and rotating the turntable between each stripe so that you begin each stripe at the south position, continue to pipe stripes, snug up against one another, until the sides of the cake are completely covered.

Piece of Cake

If you're short on time, pastry bags, star tips or food coloring, you can execute these cakes in just one icing color.

Up Your Game

Stripe the pastry bags with more than one icing color (see page 50) for a subtle and complex variation in hue within each star or stripe.

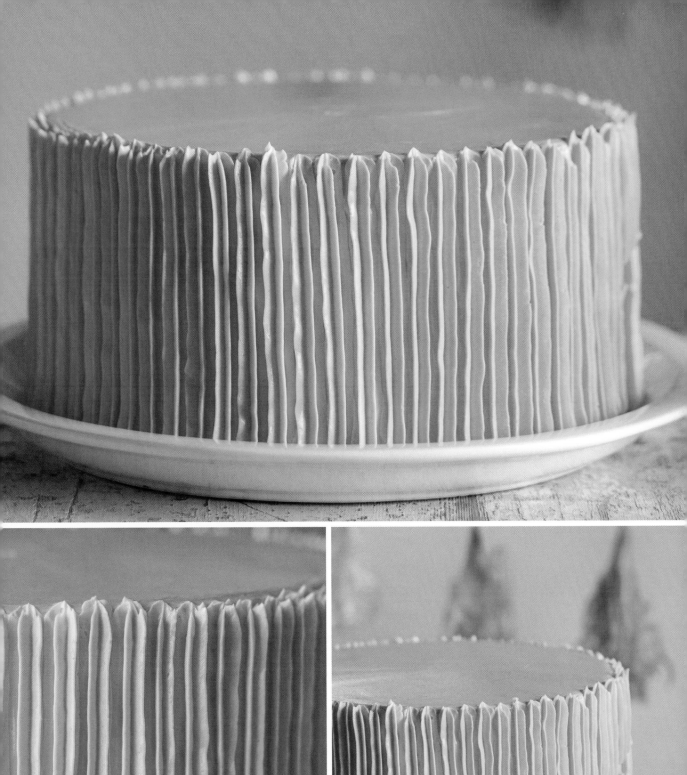

Streamer

An update on the popular ruffle decoration, this cake is the fashionista of the dessert world: effortlessly chic in stripped-down and streamlined ruffles, with an unexpected union of sweet and contemporary.

Cake: 6-inch (15 cm) cake, roughly iced (see Phraseology, page 61) in dark rose

Pastry Bags: 1 bag, fitted with a coupler

Tips: #3 rose tip

Buttercream: 1½ cups (375 mL) soft rose
2 cups (500 mL) medium rose
2 cups (500 mL) dark rose

Other Stuff: Corn syrup

Bag Prep: Fit the pastry bag with the rose tip and fill it with soft rose icing.

Cake Prep: Center the cake on the presentation surface, securing it with a dribble of corn syrup, and place it in the center of the turntable.

Learn from My Mistakes

Give your buttercream a good stir just before starting and during this project. Because piping a continuous ribbon of icing requires a supernaturally steady hand, the streamer is bound to have occasional breaks and fissures. Starting with smooth icing will minimize these hiccups.

Piece of Cake

If, while piping the streamer around the side of the cake, you found yourself holding your breath and your knuckles turned white, relax and give yourself a break by leaving the top plain. Just make sure there's enough icing on top to fully cover the cake.

New Trick: Buttercream Ribbon Spiral

This technique may look intricate, but it's actually just one long buttercream ribbon.

1. Fit a pastry bag with a rose tip and fill it with icing. Hold the bag at the South (S) position, about $\frac{1}{4}$ inch (5 mm) up from the base of the cake, with the wide side of the tip touching the cake and the narrow side pointing toward you. The bag should be nearly parallel to the turntable but with the tip at a slight downward slant. Tilt the bag sideways to a 45-degree angle.

2. Keeping your hand steady, squeeze the bag with consistent and confident pressure while rotating the turntable. Allow the ribbon to unfurl nearly parallel with the turntable. It should remain relatively straight and unruffled.

3. Continue through one full rotation of the turntable, then spiral the ribbon up about $\frac{1}{8}$ to $\frac{1}{4}$ inch (3 to 5 mm) and begin another rotation.

4. Continue spiraling up the cake until the sides of the cake are completely covered.

Decorating Steps

Using the soft rose icing, begin a buttercream ribbon spiral (see New Trick, above).

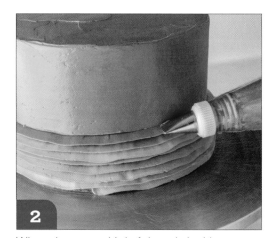

When about one-third of the cake's sides are covered, empty the remaining soft rose icing into its bowl and refill the bag with medium rose icing. Starting where you left off, continue the ribbon spiral.

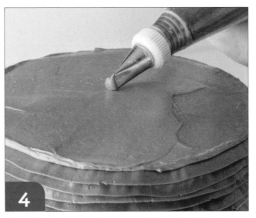

3 When about two-thirds of the cake's sides are covered, empty the remaining medium rose icing into its bowl and refill the bag with dark rose icing. Starting where you left off, continue the ribbon spiral to the top of the cake.

4 Switch back to medium rose icing. Hold the bag in the center of the cake at a 45-degree angle in the 4 o'clock direction, with the wide side of the tip touching the cake and the narrow side pointing up.

5 Rotating the turntable, begin unfurling a tight spiral of buttercream ribbon. As the spiral gets larger, it will become easier to hold the tip vertical, for a thin, upright ribbon effect.

6 When about half of the top is covered, switch back to dark rose icing. Starting where you left off, continue the spiral until you have nearly reached the edge of the cake.

7 As you approach the edge, turn the bag so that the narrow side of the tip points out and lies nearly horizontal, to create a visual transition between the horizontal ribbons on the side and the vertical ones on top.

8 Make one or two passes around the edge of the cake at this new angle until the rough coat of icing is entirely covered and there's a pleasing transition between the sides and top of the cake.

Bits & Nibbles

- This cake is best decorated in a state of light hypnosis. I hesitate to mention this, because I wouldn't want you to overthink things, but as the ribbon unfurls, it is best to keep the layers about ⅛ to ¼ inch (3 to 5 mm) apart. Avoid digging the tip into the previous layer or jumping too high and leaving a gaping space between layers. Now forget everything I just said and spin that turntable like nothing depends on it.

- Although we're forgoing the classic ruched ruffle and the up-and-down motion of the hand that creates it, you will not be able to avoid the occasional quiver and hiccup of your hand and the resulting wave in the ribbon.

- Digging the tip into the ribbon layer below is bad news, but digging it into the rough coat of icing is perfectly acceptable. Burrowing the fat end of the rose tip into the icing as you spin will keep you feeling safe and secure and keep the ribbon from leaping off the cake entirely.

- If your hand becomes fatigued, tighten your grip on the bag so that the bag does more of the work, or take a break and make note of your progress or take a slow sip of wine. In other words, feel free to pause at any time. You can start where you left off without any significant impact on the decoration.

- Each time you refill the bag between colors, squeeze a little bit of the new color out of the bag and into the bowl to release any air bubbles.

- This cake would look smashing in shades of deepest blue. Think navy, midnight and indigo.

Petals

True flower petals are brightly colored and unusually shaped to attract pollinators. With this cake, the attraction is intended for those who are keen to consume, not propagate. The purple hues chosen here are appropriately named after the prettiest collection of petals around, the orchid.

Cake: 6-inch (15 cm) cake, iced in dark orchid, roughly iced on the sides (see Phraseology, page 61) and with a Polished finish (page 59) on top

Pastry Bags: 3 bags, fitted with couplers

Buttercream: 2 cups (500 mL) light orchid
2 cups (500 mL) medium orchid
2 cups (500 mL) dark orchid

Other Stuff: Corn syrup
Small offset spatula
Damp kitchen towel

Bag Prep: Fill each pastry bag with one of the three icing colors.

Cake Prep: Center the cake on the presentation surface, securing it with a dribble of corn syrup, and place it in the center of the turntable.

Up Your Game

Use six colors of differing hues instead of three of the same hue, for a fun rainbow effect.

Bits & Nibbles

- Many of the projects in this book that require a repetitive motion have a rhythm and speed of their own. Your first couple of lines might be crooked, your dots uneven in size, and the tapering tails of different length. Once you get into an uninterrupted rhythm, things will become smoother and more uniform.

- I've seen this project executed with a spoon instead of an offset spatula. Experiment and discover which tool works best for you.

Piece of Cake

The texture of this cake is so fabulous, it doesn't require three colors for impact. Use a single color to simplify the project.

Decorating Steps

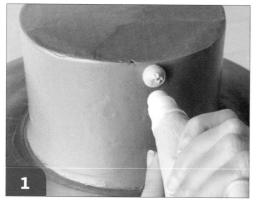

1 Using the light orchid icing, pipe a coupler dot (see New Trick, page 156) on the side of the cake at the top edge.

2 Make a second dot of light orchid icing directly below the first.

3 Using the medium orchid icing, pipe 2 more coupler dots in a line beneath the light orchid dots.

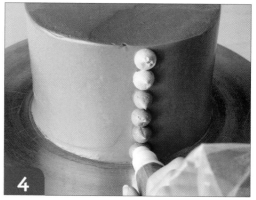

4 Using the dark orchid icing, pipe 2 more coupler dots in a line beneath the medium orchid dots, completing the vertical line of connecting dots from the top of the cake to the bottom.

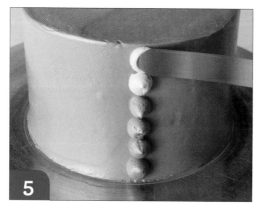

5 Hold the offset spatula facing you and nearly horizontal, with the tip resting on the center of the top dot.

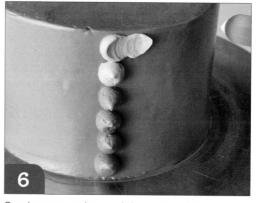

6 Gently press and spread the center of the dot horizontally 1 inch (2.5 cm) along the side of the cake, leaving a small crescent of the dot intact and creating a tapering tail.

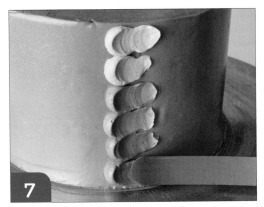

7

Working down the line, repeat step 6 with all of the dots, cleaning the spatula with a damp kitchen towel in between dots.

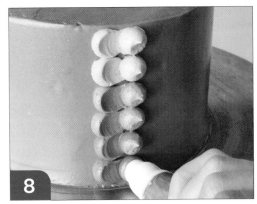

8

Make another line of dots, in the same colors, down the side of the cake, placing each new dot on top of the tapering tail of a dot in the first line, about ½ inch (1 cm) from the crescent.

9

Repeat step 6 down the second line of dots.

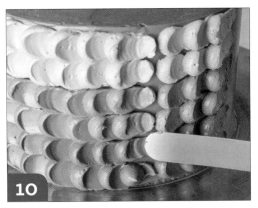

10

Continue to pipe and spread vertical lines of dots until you have circled the cake and are almost back where you began.

11

Because there is no way to spread the tails of the last line of dots under the first, we will create an optical illusion. Pipe the last line of vertical dots next to the crescents in the first line.

12

Wet the tip of your index finger and make a slight indentation in each dot, mimicking the indentation made by the spatula.

Wintertide

Ombré cakes usually play with the saturation level of just one color, but this sophisticated number shifts between multiple hues. Intense and soulful, the muted tones of this cake evoke introspective gray days of yellowing lawns and the pressing tidal shift into winter.

Cake: 8-inch (20 cm) cake, crumb-coated or roughly iced (see Phraseology, page 61) in soft chartreuse

Pastry Bags: 1 bag, fitted with a coupler

Buttercream: 2 cups (500 mL) dark gray-blue
2 cups (500 mL) medium gray-blue
2 cups (500 mL) teal
3 cups (750 mL) moss green
4 cups (1 L) soft chartreuse

Other Stuff: Corn syrup
Straight spatula
Large rectangular comb with a straight edge
Large offset spatula
Damp kitchen towel

Bag Prep: Fill the pastry bag with dark gray-blue icing.

Cake Prep: Make sure the cake is in the center of the turntable. (Do not transfer it to your presentation surface until after you have completed the decorating steps.)

Piece of Cake

This cake doesn't necessarily need to be iced as smooth as a pebble. Make the sides of the cake relatively vertical and the top approximately level, and let the finish be rough and free, similar to a Lath and Plaster finish (page 64).

If you think you may become weary of swapping out colors, you can reduce the number of colors to three and pipe two stripes of each. You can also just use one color for the top of the cake.

Decorating Steps

1 Hold the bag of dark gray-blue icing nearly horizontal at the South (S) position at the base of the cake, with the coupler ¼ inch (5 mm) from the surface of the cake.

2 Squeeze the bag with firm pressure as you rotate the turntable, creating a stripe of icing around the base of the cake.

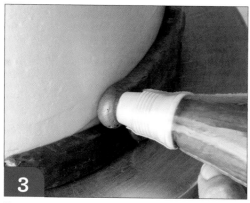

3 Empty the remaining dark gray-blue icing into its bowl and refill the bag with medium gray-blue icing. Pipe a second stripe of icing directly above the first.

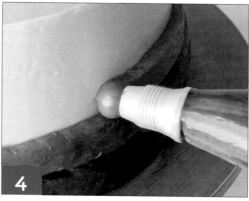

4 Empty the remaining medium gray-blue icing into its bowl and refill the bag with teal icing. Pipe a third stripe of icing directly above the second.

5 Switch from teal to moss green icing and pipe a fourth stripe above the third.

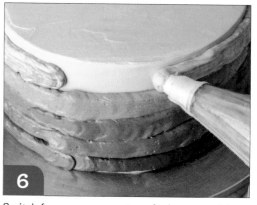

6 Switch from moss green to soft chartreuse icing and pipe a fifth stripe above the fourth.

7

If there is still crumb coating visible above the chartreuse stripe, pipe a second chartreuse stripe. It's okay if this last stripe rises slightly above the top of the cake.

8

Still using chartreuse icing, begin to pipe rings of icing on the top of the cake, working from the outside toward the center.

9

When about half of the top is covered, switch back to moss green icing. Continue piping rings until the top of the cake is covered.

10

Follow steps 3 to 4 and steps 9 to 14 of Polished (pages 60 and 62–63) to smooth the top and sides of the cake.

Bits & Nibbles

- Because the pastry bag is held quite close to the cake in this project, the stripes piped in steps 1 to 7 will not be tubular like the opening of the coupler but flatter and thinner.

- Each time you refill the bag between colors, squeeze a little bit of the new color out of the bag and into the bowl to release any air bubbles.

- Because you are using one bag for all the colors, the beginning of every stripe will be a mixture of the old color and the new. This is not only acceptable, it's preferable: the subtle blending of colors makes for a more interesting and evocative cake.

Up Your Game

Want more variation on top of your cake? Pipe rings of multiple colors instead of just two.

Giving a Fig

The fig is the fruity embodiment of all that is feminine and sumptuous, the expanding raindrop silhouette of a half-cheeked Rubenesque torso. When I eat cake, I feel decadent, and when eating a fig, I inhale an idle Mediterranean moment. Paired with glittering crystallized blueberries and blackberries, this cake brings together the best of summer's bounty. Explore your local farmers' market or produce aisle and find seasonal inspiration for your next cake.

Cake: 8-inch (20 cm) cake, crumb-coated in light purple icing

Pastry Bags: 2 bags, fitted with couplers

Tips: Any medium round tip (a #4 works well)

Buttercream: 1½ cups (375 mL) deep purple
3 cups (750 mL) pale purple
1½ cups (375 mL) dark purple
1½ cups (375 mL) medium purple
1½ cups (375 mL) light purple

Other Stuff: Corn syrup
3 stems of hard round florist's berries
Small carton of blueberries, crystallized (see New Trick, page 180)
Small carton of blackberries, crystallized
1 egg white
Superfine sugar
Small, thin paintbrush
Parchment paper
3 Black Mission or Brown Turkey figs, cut in half lengthwise
Toothpicks
1 bar of quality white chocolate, chopped into rough angular chunks

Bag Prep: Leave one of the pastry bags without a tip and fill it with the deep purple icing. Fit the other bag with the round tip and fill it with ½ cup (125 mL) of the pale purple icing.

Cake Prep: Center the cake on the presentation surface, securing it with a dribble of corn syrup, and place it in the center of the turntable. Starting with deep purple icing, ice the sides of the cake in ombré purple, following steps 1 to 7 of Wintertide (pages 176–177) and changing to the next lighter shade of purple after each stripe. Working from the outside toward the center, pipe rings of pale purple icing over the top of the cake. Follow steps 3 to 4 and steps 9 to 14 of Polished (pages 60 and 62–63) to smooth the top and sides of the cake.

New Trick: Crystallizing Berries

Use this easy technique to add glittering elegance to your cake.

1 Wash the berries and let them dry completely. Separate an egg white into a small bowl, and place a small bowl of superfine sugar nearby.

2 Using a small, thin paintbrush, brush part of a berry with a thin wash of egg white.

3 Dip the portion of the berry brushed with egg into the bowl of sugar.

4 As they are dipped, set each berry, sugar side up, on a sheet of parchment paper. Let dry for about 30 minutes.

Cake Debate

Q: Dear Carey, I feel like I'm being plagued by a pack of flying blue monkeys, because the sugar on my crystallized berries is melting like the Wicked Witch of the West. What am I doing wrong?

Sincerely, Clicking My Heels to No Avail

A: Dear CMHTNA, Your metaphor is spot-on, because the very substance that caused the Wicked Witch to melt — water! — is the same scourge that is melting your sugar. Water will melt sugar, but a thin layer of egg white will not. Make sure your berries are thoroughly dry before beginning the crystallization process.

Decorating Steps

1

Separate small sprigs of florist's berries from their stems. Wash the berries and let them dry completely.

2

Arrange 5 fig halves on top of the cake, spacing them evenly around the perimeter. Place them at different angles and secure them with toothpicks. (Eat the remaining fig half.)

3

Using light purple icing as glue, tuck a crystallized blackberry next to each fig. Place a crystallized blueberry on the opposite side of each fig.

4

Begin to tuck sprigs of berries around each cluster of fruit.

5

Add a chunk or two of white chocolate to each cluster.

6

Fill in any gaps with more blackberries, blueberries, florist's berries and chocolate until the decorations are visually balanced.

Bits & Nibbles

- Gently dry berries by lining a baking sheet with cushy layers of paper towels. Grasp the pan on each side and gently shake it from side to side, rolling the berries around the pan.

- Remember to remove all inedible plants and props from the cake before serving it. Worried about the visual massacre that will remain after you have removed the decorations? Display your lovely cake as guests arrive, then, when it is time to serve, carry the cake to the kitchen, slice and plate individual pieces and sprinkle them with cut fruit, berries and white chocolate shavings.

- Evenly distributing the fruit in steps 2 and 3 creates visual focal points and gives the cake a pleasant balanced appearance.

Piece of Cake

If you don't plan to travel with your cake and you have the smooth, practiced gait of a Southern debutante, skip the toothpicks and icing glue and just rest your decorations on top of the cake.

Short on time? Skip crystallizing the fruit.

Up Your Game

Prefer a brimming fruit-filled wreath to crown your cake? Start piling and layering the fruit using toothpicks and skewers as structural support. Fill in gaps with smaller fruits and chocolate pieces for additional buttressing.

Chapter 7

Buttercream Blossoms

Flowers illustrate all the best aspects of decorating with buttercream. They can be simple and stylized like a daisy, delicate and plump like a ribbon rose or naturalistic and soaring like a cactus. Although I know buttercream was originally concocted for eating, I sometimes think its greatest use is for piping flowers.

Groovy

This daisy cake has enough funk for the inner flower child to get her groove on, but the sophisticated color palette satisfies our grown-up sensibilities.

Cake: 6-inch (15 cm) cake, iced in teal with a Polished finish (page 59)

Pastry Bags: 5 bags, 2 fitted with couplers

Tips: #126 rose tip
Two #124 rose tips
Two #12 round tips

Buttercream: 1½ cups (375 mL) orange
1½ cups (375 mL) soft periwinkle
1½ cups (375 mL) yellow
¼ cup (60 mL) white
¼ cup (60 mL) black

Other Stuff: Corn syrup

Bag Prep: Fit the #126 rose tip and the #124 rose tips onto pastry bags without couplers. Fit the #12 round tips onto bags with couplers. Fill the bags accordingly:
- #126 rose tip: orange icing
- #124 rose tip: soft periwinkle icing
- #124 rose tip: yellow icing
- #12 round tip: white icing
- #12 round tip: black icing

Cake Prep: Center the cake on the presentation surface, securing it with a dribble of corn syrup, and place it in the center of the turntable.

New Trick: Drop Petal Daisy

Daisy petals are really no more than elongated dots, made with a rose tip instead of a round tip, and the technique for piping them is just the same. Piping daisies simply involves piping a ring of petals around a center point, then piping a dot in the center.

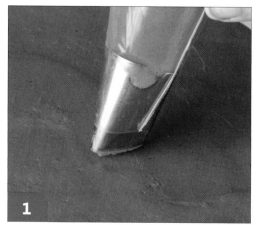

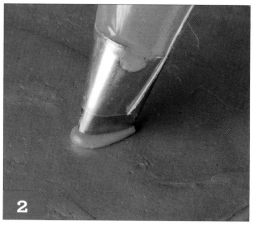

Fit a pastry bag with a rose tip and fill it with icing. Hold the bag so that the opening of the rose tip is parallel to the surface of the cake and is hovering just above or in front of it.

Squeeze the bag with moderate pressure until the icing begins to balloon out from the tip. Stop squeezing when the icing threatens to engulf the opening of the tip. Release pressure completely before moving the bag away.

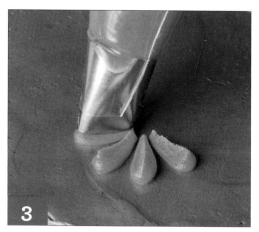

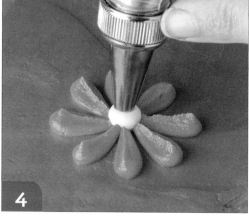

Keeping your hand in place and the bag hovering just above the cake, rotate the turntable slightly and pipe a second petal next to the first. Continue piping petals in a ring, rotating the turntable slightly between each.

Fit another pastry bag with a round tip and fill it with icing in a contrasting color. Pipe a dot in the center of the daisy. Wet the tip of your index finger and gently tap down and round the dot.

Bits & Nibbles

- Here are a few tricks to ensure that your daisies are relatively round:

1. When piping a daisy on top of a cake, hold the pastry bag in the 11 o'clock direction, with the decorating tip ¼ inch (5 mm) from the surface of the cake and the narrow end of the opening pointing toward the center of your daisy. Hold your hand firmly in place and allow a slight rotation of the turntable in between each petal to take the guesswork out of where and at what angle the next petal should be placed. (When piping a daisy on the side of a cake, you won't be able to rely on rotating the turntable to place the petals, so you will have to become comfortable with unfamiliar wrist angles and flipping the bag upside down to achieve different petal angles.)

2. Use a small cap (or anything small and round) to make an impression slightly larger than the dot you will pipe in the center of the flower. This impression will be your guide, showing you where to place the pointy end of each petal.

3. If you find it challenging to space the petals evenly, try piping them in pairs. After piping the first petal, pipe the second petal directly across the center from it, mirroring it. Pipe the third petal halfway in between the first and second petals, and the fourth petal directly opposite the third petal, essentially creating a petal-shaped plus sign. Fill in the gaps with mirrored pairs of petals.

- Drop petal daisies might have anywhere from 5 to 10 petals — it's up to you!

Piece of Cake

For less work but equal flower power, pipe a sinuous river of daisies that starts wide on the side of the cake and tapers up and over onto the top.

This cake is equally compelling with a more limited color palette. Imagine a soft blue cake for a shower, covered with pale yellow daisies with soft brown centers, or an autumn-themed cake with chocolate icing and orange daisies with yellow centers.

Decorating Steps

1. Using the orange icing, pipe a drop petal daisy (see New Trick, page 188) on top of the cake, in any location.

2. Using the periwinkle icing, pipe a half daisy on top of the cake, near the edge. Start by piping 2 petals that hug the edge of the cake, then fill in the remaining petals.

3. Finish the periwinkle daisy by piping 3 to 4 petals on the side of the cake, directly below the petals on top of the cake.

4. Using the yellow icing, pipe a yellow daisy on the side of the cake, near the periwinkle daisy.

5. Rotating among the three colors, continue piping daisies around the cake, completely covering the top and sides. When working near the bottom of the cake, pipe half daisies.

6. Using white icing for the orange daisies and black icing for the other daisies, pipe a fat dot in the center of each daisy. Wet the tip of your index finger and gently tap down and round each dot.

Sakura

Due to their fleeting nature and their proclivity to bloom en masse, cherry blossoms, or sakura in Japanese, symbolize clouds. The blossoms on this cake reflect the same ephemeral delicacy, and the delectability of the cake ensures an equally fleeting lifespan.

Cake: 6-inch (15 cm) cake, iced in soft moss green with a Polished finish (page 59) and chilled

Pastry Bags: 3 bags, fitted with couplers

Tips: #3 round tip, #6 round tip, #59 petal tip or #102 rose tip

Buttercream: 1/3 cup (75 mL) soft moss green
1/4 cup (60 mL) medium beige
1/3 cup (75 mL) light beige
1/2 cup (125 mL) soft pink
1 1/2 cups (375 mL) white

Other Stuff: Corn syrup
22 inches (55 cm) green-and-white gingham ribbon
22 inches (55 cm) coordinating rickrack ribbon
Toothpick or skewer
Tweezers (optional)
Pink nonpareils

> ## Phraseology
>
> *Rickrack:* A narrow ribbon with a zigzag silhouette, rickrack has a fun shape and a nostalgic vintage feel.

Bag Prep: Fit each of the tips onto a pastry bag. Fill the bags accordingly:
- #3 round tip: moss green icing
- #6 round tip: stripe the bag with medium beige icing (see page 50), then fill it with light beige icing
- #59 petal tip: stripe the bag with soft pink icing, then fill it with white icing

Cake Prep: Center the cake on the presentation surface, securing it with a dribble of corn syrup, and place it in the center of the turntable.

New Trick: Five-Petal Flower

A five-petal flower is a handy flower to have in your toolbox. Pipe it in soft pink with a darker pink center, and you have a cherry blossom. Pipe it in purple with a yellow center, and you have a violet. Pipe a pile of petals in white, and you've created a hydrangea.

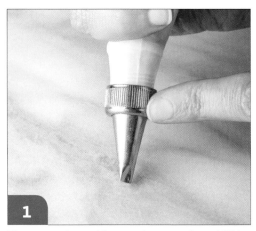

1

Fit a pastry bag with a petal or rose tip and fill it with icing. Hold the bag at a 45-degree angle to the surface, with the wide end nearer to you and lightly touching the surface, and the narrow end pointed away from you and hovering just above the surface.

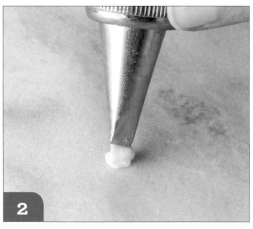

2

Squeeze the bag with moderate pressure to build an anchor of icing.

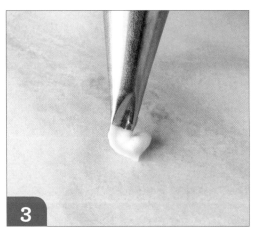

3

Move the tip slightly up and away from you while slowly and slightly spinning the turntable counterclockwise.

4

Continue to spin the turntable as you return the tip to the starting point. Release pressure before moving the tip away.

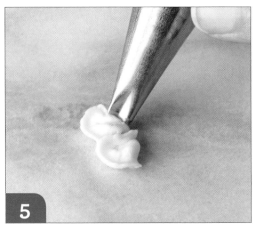

5

Spin the turntable slightly and pipe a second petal snugly next to the first.

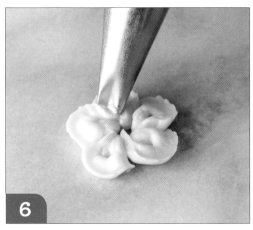

6

Pipe 3 more petals next to one another to complete the flower, spinning the turntable slightly between each petal. Pipe a dot or sprinkle nonpareils into the center.

New Trick: Drop Blossoms and Buds

The tiny blossoms featured on this cake are miniscule five-petal daisies dressed up in pink and white. See page 188 for detailed instructions on piping a daisy. Making a bud is a simple matter of piping a single petal.

Decorating Steps

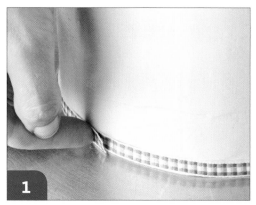

1

Affix the gingham ribbon around the bottom of the cake (see New Trick, page 90), securing it with a little dab of moss green icing.

2

Affix the rickrack ribbon around the cake, just above the gingham ribbon.

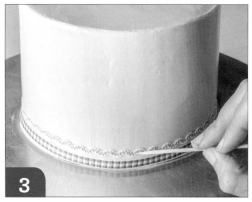

3

Using the toothpick, gently nudge the rickrack ribbon to an equal distance from the gingham ribbon around the entire cake.

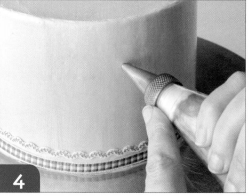

4

Hold the bag of beige icing perpendicular to the side of the cake, about 1 inch (2.5 cm) below the top edge, with the tip hovering just off the surface.

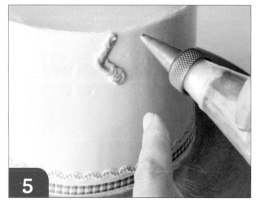

5

Pipe a fat sideways V to the top edge of the cake, allowing the icing to balloon out and ripple under the tip as you move your hand.

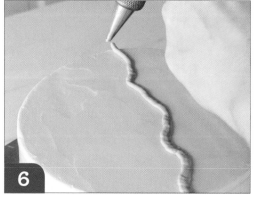

6

Starting from the tip of the V on the top edge, pipe a fat, wavy beige line across the top of the cake, allowing the line to taper as it nears the far side.

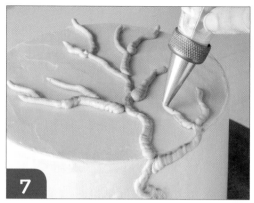

7

Pipe rippled offshoots from the main branch, tapering them to get smaller and thinner the farther they get from the main branch.

8

Using the striped pink and white icing, pipe five-petal flowers (see New Trick, page 194) on and around the branches, piping them individually and in clusters, with fewer flowers near the ends of the branches.

9

Pipe small drop blossoms and buds (see New Trick, page 195), scattering them around the branches but concentrating them near the tips of the branches.

10

Use your fingertips or tweezers to drop a random number of pink nonpareils into the center of each blossom.

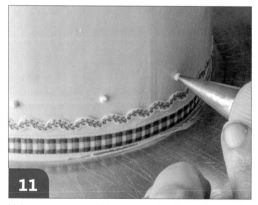

11

Using moss green icing, pipe a horizontal row of evenly spaced dots around the base of the cake, just above the rickrack ribbon.

12

Pipe a horizontal row of evenly spaced dots around the top edge of the cake, lining each dot up vertically with a dot piped below.

13 Pipe a horizontal row of evenly spaced dots halfway in between the top and bottom dots, ensuring that the dots in all three rows are vertically aligned.

14 The rows of stacked dots create an illusion of 2 empty squares, one on top of the other. Pipe a dot in the center of each square.

Bits & Nibbles

- To keep the petals aligned and the flowers round when piping five-petal flowers, pipe each petal evenly spaced around an imaginary circle the size of an eraser tip. Alternatively, you can use a toothpick to actually draw a tiny circle on the surface of the cake as a guide.

- The dot pattern piped onto the sides of the cake in steps 11 to 14 is known as Swiss dots. If while piping Swiss dots you come across a branch smack-dab in the place where a dot should be, skip that dot. Ensure that the previous dot and the next one are aligned with the dots below.

Desert Rose

If you prize the cactus for its dramatic beauty and for requiring little upkeep as a houseplant, then you'll love this cake for the same reasons. There's nothing harsh and unforgiving about this desert. Succulents have never been so succulent!

Cake: 8-inch (20 cm) cake, iced in soft terracotta with a Lath and Plaster finish (page 64)

Pastry Bags: 4 bags, fitted with couplers

Tips: #32 or similar open star tip
#1 round tip
#16 or similar star tip

Buttercream: 3 cups (750 mL) medium grass green
¼ cup (60 mL) yellow buttercream
⅓ cup (75 mL) white
⅓ cup (75 mL) bright pink

Other Stuff: Corn syrup

Bag Prep: Fit each of the tips onto a pastry bag, leaving one bag without a tip. Fill the bags accordingly:
- Coupler only: 2 cups (500 mL) medium grass green icing
- #32 open star tip: stripe the bag with yellow icing (see page 50), then fill it with the remaining green icing
- #1 round tip: white icing
- #16 star tip: bright pink icing

Cake Prep: Center the cake on the presentation surface, securing it with a dribble of corn syrup, and place it in the center of the turntable.

New Trick: Drop Flowers

1. Fit a pastry bag with a drop flower or star tip and fill it with icing. Hover the tip just above the cake (if piping the flower on top) or in front of the cake (if piping the flower on the side) and squeeze the bag with moderate pressure until the icing just begins to envelop the tip.

2. Completely release pressure on the bag before slowly moving it away to the side.

Decorating Steps

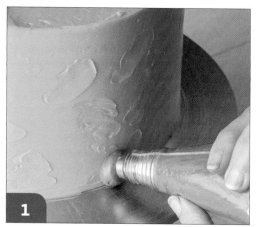

Hold the bag of unstriped green icing at the bottom of the cake, parallel to the turntable and with the coupler ¼ to ⅓ inch (5 to 8 mm) from the surface of the cake. Squeeze the bag to anchor the icing to the cake.

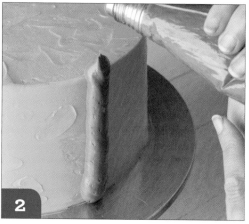

Continue to squeeze with even pressure while drawing your hand up, creating a fat line up the side of the cake. When you reach the top, stop squeezing but continue moving your hand upward, creating a fat taper.

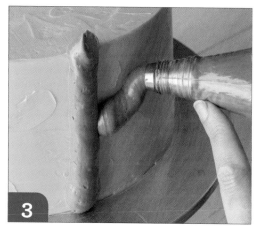

Pipe an arm on either side of the cactus, sprouting from near the middle, with one arm slightly lower and larger than the other.

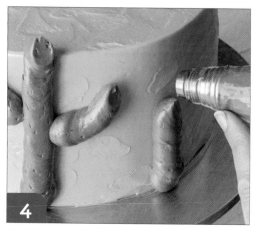

Pipe 3 or 4 similar cacti of random sizes and shapes around the cake, circling halfway around the sides.

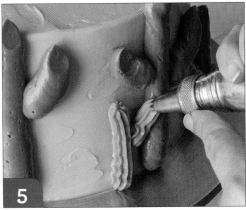

5

Using the striped yellow and green icing, pipe 4 or 5 smaller cacti around the large green cacti, overlapping them at times.

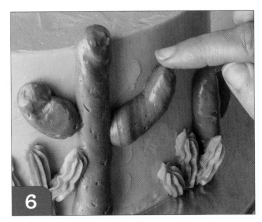

6

Wet the tip of your index finger and gently tap down and round any points or angles on the cacti.

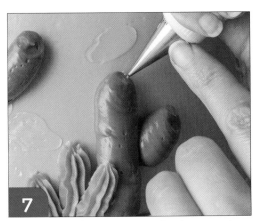

7

Hold the bag of white icing so that it grazes the surface of a large green cactus, steadying it with a finger from your other hand.

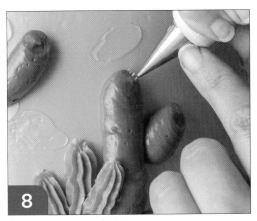

8

Squeeze the bag with firm pressure so that the icing anchors to the cactus. Pull the bag away while decreasing the pressure, allowing the icing to break off into a tiny spike.

9

Pipe lengthwise lines of spikes over all the large green cacti until they are fully covered.

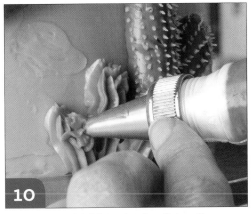

10

Using bright pink icing, pipe 1 or 2 drop flowers (see New Trick, page 202) onto each of the smaller cacti.

Bits & Nibbles

- When making cacti, you want them to remain as fat and round as possible. This means holding the coupler or tip at a consistent distance from the cake while piping. If you hold the coupler or tip too close to the cake, the icing will compress and your cacti could end up looking like Gumby.

- When making the larger cacti, allow some of them to run up to and past the top of the cake.

- This cake is directional, meaning that the cacti are piped only halfway around the sides. Feel free to pipe cacti around the entire cake. (Doing so will also allow for a strategic rotation of the cake that will showcase your best work.)

- Cactus spikes can be as pernicious in icing as they are in real life. When you first start piping spikes, you may end up with more stuck to the end of your decorating tip than to the cactus. Don't lose faith; with a little practice, you'll be piping spikes on autopilot.

Piece of Cake

Forgo the more perilous vertical piping on the side of the cake and instead create a cactus vignette on top. You can even add graham cracker crumbs to stand in for sand.

Lilacs

For its beauty and ease, this is hands down one of my favorite cakes. I rely on lilacs whenever I need a cake that is fast and easy but with high impact. Lilacs are also valuable for their ability to conceal hasty icing jobs or a misplaced thumb jab into the icing.

Cake: 6-inch (15 cm) cake, iced in warm magenta with a Polished finish (page 59)

Pastry Bags: 4 bags, fitted with couplers

Tips: #70 or similar leaf tip
Three #131 or similar drop flower tips

Buttercream: 1 cup (250 mL) grass green
2 cups (500 mL) lavender
2 cups (500 mL) grape
2 cups (500 mL) soft periwinkle

Other Stuff: Corn syrup

Bag Prep: Fit each of the tips onto a pastry bag. Fill the bags accordingly:
- #70 leaf tip: grass green icing
- #131 drop flower tip: stripe the bag with lavender or grape icing (see page 50), then fill it with periwinkle icing
- #131 drop flower tip: stripe the bag with grape or periwinkle icing, then fill it with lavender icing
- #131 drop flower tip: stripe the bag with periwinkle or lavender icing, then fill it with grape icing

Cake Prep: Center the cake on the presentation surface, securing it with a dribble of corn syrup, and place it in the center of the turntable.

New Trick: Buttercream Leaves

In addition to depth and dimension, leaves add naturalism to a cake. The Lilacs cake might look like drooping bunches of buttercream fluff if it weren't for the obvious green pop of the leaves. Pipe with adequate pressure and a master cake decorator's confidence to avoid leaves that are thin, narrow and anemic. You can make leaves in any direction, but it might be easiest to first practice leaves that go from left to right.

1. Fit a pastry bag with a leaf tip and fill it with icing. Hold the bag at a 45-degree angle to the surface of the cake. With the tip touching the surface, squeeze the bag and, while moving the bag away from your starting point, increase the pressure so that the leaf balloons out at the base.

2. Still moving your hand away from your starting point, decrease the pressure, allowing the leaf to begin tapering. Continue to move your hand out and away as you stop squeezing. This follow-through will give the leaf a nice taper.

The technique is similar if you want to pipe a leaf that rises vertically from the top of the cake. Hold the bag nearly vertical, with the tip touching the surface. Squeeze the bag to anchor the icing. Still squeezing, move your hand up to create the fat base of the leaf. Begin to decrease pressure, allowing the leaf to taper. Continue to move your hand up and away as you stop squeezing.

Decorating Steps

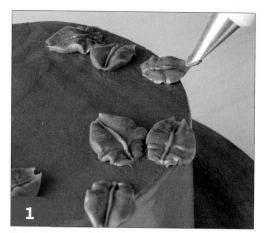

1

Using the green icing, pipe randomly placed leaves (see New Trick, above) around the top perimeter of the cake, with some pointing out and some pointing in. Pipe both individual leaves and sets of leaves.

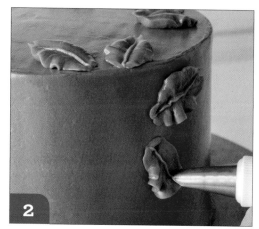

2

Pipe leaves here and there around the side of the cake, near the top.

Using any of the purple icings, begin to pipe drop flowers (see New Trick, page 202) that overlap the edges of some of the leaves on top of the cake.

Continue to pipe drop flowers to create the rough outline of a lilac cluster that starts on top of the cake and cascades over the edge, tapering at the end.

Fill in the cluster by overlapping and layering drop flowers, making the cluster fuller at the top and narrow and thin as it reaches the bottom.

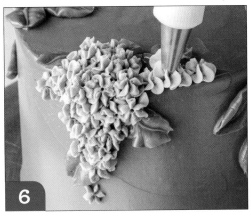

Using a different purple icing, begin piping a second lilac cluster next to the first, allowing the clusters to butt up against each other on top of the cake.

As you outline and fill in the second cluster down the side of the cake, taper its tail in a different direction from the first cluster and end it at a different length.

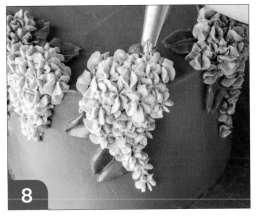

Alternating among the three purple icings, continue to pipe lilac clusters around the top and sides of the cake. Pipe some clusters individually and others in pairs.

Using green icing, pipe a few vertical leaves rising from the top of the lilac clusters.

Pipe a few lilac blossoms around the base of each vertical leaf, making it appear to be embedded within the cluster.

Bits & Nibbles

- Feel free to use any leaf tip to make the leaves on this cake, but I recommend steering clear of those that are tiny. Small tips make for squirrelly, unmanageable buttercream.

- If your leaves are ruffled, it indicates that you are squeezing the bag with a good deal of pressure but are not moving your hand at an equivalent rate of speed, causing the buttercream to back up. To remedy this, you can squeeze with less pressure or move your hand faster — or you can come to appreciate ruffled leaves.

- When choosing where to pipe a lilac cluster, pick a spot that will allow some leaves to poke out from underneath the flowers.

- Pipe lilac clusters that vary in length, width, direction and fullness.

Piece of Cake

This cake is charming iced in white and with lilac clusters in just one deep purple color. Stripe the bag with white to add dimension and variety to the blooms.

Ribbon Roses

Ribbon roses consist of one or two continuous ribbons of buttercream, rather than the layered petals of standard buttercream roses. There is something sweet and beguiling to their simplicity, especially when they are paired with fluttery ribbon fragments in pastel colors.

Cake: 6-inch (15 cm) cake, iced in white with a Lath and Plaster finish (page 64) and chilled

Pastry Bags: 4 pastry bags, 3 fitted with couplers

Tips: #352 leaf tip
#104 rose tip
#103 rose tip
#124 rose tip

Buttercream: 1/2 cup (125 mL) white
2 cups (500 mL) pale mint green
2 cups (500 mL) light beige
2 1/2 cups (625 mL) soft peach

Other Stuff: Squeeze bottle of corn syrup
22 inches (55 cm) wide burlap ribbon
22 inches (55 cm) thin gold ribbon
Multiple pieces of thin pastel ribbons, trim and lace, each 2 to 4 inches (5 to 10 cm) long
#9 or similar rose nail
Small scissors

Bag Prep: Fit the #352 leaf tip, the #104 rose tip and the #103 rose tip onto the pastry bags with couplers. Fit the #124 rose tip onto the remaining bag. Fill the bags accordingly:
- #352 leaf tip: white icing
- #104 rose tip: pale mint green icing
- #103 rose tip: light beige icing
- #124 rose tip: soft peach icing

Cake Prep: Center the cake on the presentation surface, securing it with a dribble of corn syrup, and place it in the center of the turntable.

New Trick: Ribbon Roses and Buds

The difference between a ribbon rose and a ribbon bud is simply the angle of your decorating tip and how many layers of buttercream you choose to add. When you're making a bud, the tip starts nearly vertical and ends with very little adjustment to the angle. A full bloom rose will start with the tip nearly vertical and end with it almost horizontal, so that the rose is wider at the base and appears to be open.

All roses and buds start with a solid base of buttercream. Making the base is essentially the same technique used to make the rose itself, except that the bag is held at a 45-degree angle so that the tip is tilted toward the center of the rose nail, creating a buttercream cone. The sturdier your base, the more durable your rose will be when you're transferring it from the nail to the cake.

The instructions that follow are for a large ribbon rose. For a smaller rose or a bud, simply make a smaller base and wrap fewer layers of buttercream. A #104 rose tip is a good tip to practice with, as it's neither too big or too small.

Scissors are used to transfer ribbon roses and buds from the rose nail to the cake. Smaller scissors tend to be easier to manipulate.

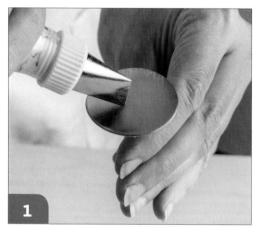

Fit a pastry bag with a rose tip and fill it with icing. Hold a rose nail between the thumb and index finger of your nondominant hand. With your other hand, hold the pastry bag at a 45-degree angle, with the fat end of the tip down.

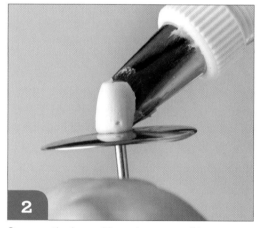

Squeeze the bag with moderate, confident pressure as you spin the rose nail to wrap the icing around itself.

Phraseology

Rose Nail: A rose nail is a small, round stainless steel disk attached to a thin nail-like shaft. A rose nail allows you to pipe flowers on a small, controllable surface that can be easily spun between your fingers. Make sure to buy rose nails with threads on the shaft. Hands tend to pick up a thin coat of grease when working with buttercream, and that coating makes a rose nail without threads almost impossible to spin.

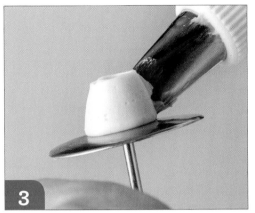

3

Keep spinning and wrapping the buttercream until you have formed a small cone of buttercream.

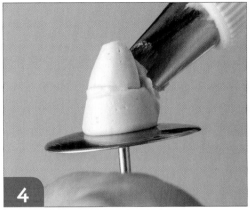

4

Using the same method, make a smaller cone of icing on top of the first.

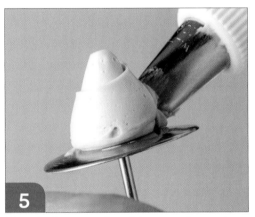

5

After the first wrapping of the second cone, draw your hand down, firmly connecting the upper and lower cones.

6

Change the angle of the bag so that the tip is nearly vertical. Squeeze the bag and spin the nail to wrap the icing around the top cone, gradually drawing your hand down until you can no longer spin the nail.

7

Alter the tip angle so that the icing ribbon tilts slightly out, as if the rose is opening, and continue to wrap layers around the base while gradually drawing your hand down and increasing the angle of the tip.

8

Tilt the nail slightly so that you can easily add the last icing ribbon. As you reach the bottom of the base, the tip should be nearly horizontal so that the bottom ribbon is open and wide.

9

With the scissors slightly open, maneuver them underneath the rose, between the rose and the nail. Close the scissors slightly so that they are still open but hug the base of the rose.

10

Lift the rose off the nail and hover the scissors just above the place where the rose will be placed on the cake. Close the scissors and pull them out from beneath the rose.

Decorating Steps

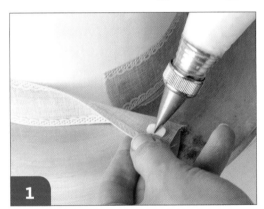

1

Affix the burlap ribbon around the bottom of the cake (see New Trick, page 90), securing it with a little dab of white icing.

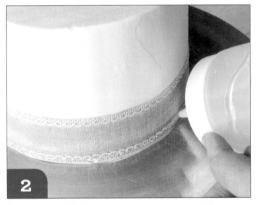

2

Squeeze a thin line of corn syrup around the bottom of the burlap ribbon.

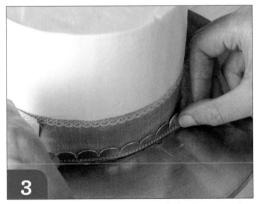

3

Wrap the thin gold ribbon around the bottom of the cake, overlapping the burlap ribbon.

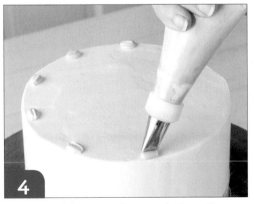

4

Using any of the pastry bags, make 8 small, evenly spaced dollops of icing around the perimeter on top of the cake.

5

Artfully affix 3 or 4 pastel ribbon pieces to each of the icing dollops.

6

Using the peach icing, pipe 4 ribbon roses of various sizes (see New Trick, page 214) and place them around the perimeter of the cake, spacing them evenly and placing them at varying angles.

7

Using the mint green icing, pipe 4 ribbon roses of various sizes and place each one next to a peach rose, at varying angles.

8

Using the beige icing, pipe ribbon roses of various sizes to fill in the major gaps between the peach and green roses.

9

Pipe peach, mint green and beige buds and place them strategically around the cake to fill in any remaining gaps.

10

Using the white icing, pipe leaves radiating out from beneath the roses, pointing the leaves in different directions.

Bits & Nibbles

- To keep the composition interesting and naturalistic, place your roses on the cake at different angles and facing in different directions. Have some facing out, some facing in and some facing each other.

- It's not a requirement to use pastel ribbon or ribbon that is similar to what is pictured. Use whatever you happen to have or like. Match the color of your roses to the selected ribbon.

Chapter 8

Cupcake Creations

The cupcake's size and simplicity belies its impact, on both the eye and stomach. Forget big, scary knives and sliding cake layers; these half-pint pastries are as simple as it gets, and there's something about their compact, personal-sized perfection that makes a heart happy.

Cupcakes may be little power-packed punches of deliciousness, but their quick, uncomplicated assembly is what makes them my go-to dessert when time is short or inertia prevails. When cake is called for but time in the kitchen feels like after-school detention, I opt for the compliant cupcake. A little color and a toss of sprinkles, and cupcakes become the ideal stand-alone dessert. Smooth them out to create bite-sized canvases for self-expression, or group them together to make a hybrid cupcake cake.

Button Top

These cupcakes are smooth and flat, and make a great base for further decoration, though I happen to think the petite platters of icing are as cute as a button (minus the holes) even without added adornment.

Cupcakes:	24 standard or mini cupcakes, cooled and leveled
Pastry Bags:	1 bag
Tips:	1 extra-large round tip (or a coupler with no tip attached)
Buttercream:	5 cups (1.25 L)
Other Stuff:	Small offset spatula Spray bottle (optional) Small plate (optional)
Bag Prep:	Fit the pastry bag with the round tip (or coupler) and fill it with about 2 cups (500 mL) icing. Refill as needed.
Cupcake Prep:	Place a cooled cupcake in the center of the turntable.

Bits & Nibbles

- Cupcakes can pop out of the oven with plump domes or conveniently flat, depending on the recipe. Leveling a domed cupcake is just like leveling a cake layer. See page 36 for detailed instructions.

- When making the rings of icing, keep the decorating tip far enough away from the cupcake that the icing can drape gracefully into its natural tubular shape.

- When smoothing the icing with the spatula, try not to remove much icing and work to keep the nicely rounded edge fully intact. Clean the spatula on the edge of a bowl between swipes.

- If you're using the alternative smoothing method and you find that some icing is sticking to the plate, add a little more water.

- For some easy bling, gently roll the edges of the iced cupcake in sprinkles or colored sugar that you have poured onto a small plate.

Decorating Steps

1

Hold the pastry bag vertically about ⅓ inch (8 mm) above the cupcake, near the edge. Squeeze the bag with moderate pressure, anchoring the icing to the cupcake.

2

Continue to squeeze the bag while moving your arm in a small circular motion so that the icing coils around the cupcake, forming a complete circle.

3

Make a second ring of icing that completely fills the center of the cupcake.

4

Pick up the cupcake and angle it slightly toward you. Holding the spatula at a 45-degree angle away from you, swipe across the icing with the thin back edge, smoothing the seams between the rings.

5

Rotate the cupcake 90 degrees and make a second swipe.

6

Continue to rotate and swipe across the cupcake until the icing is smooth and level.

Alternative (and Fun) Smoothing Method

1

After following steps 1 to 3 on page 224, use a spray bottle filled with water to spray a small plate (or dribble it with water). You need only enough water to just coat the plate.

2

Turn the cupcake upside down and gently, without squashing or deforming the shape of the icing, move the cupcake in small circles, much like using a piece of bread to sop up olive oil.

3

Flip the cupcake back over to see if the seams from the individual rings of icing have disappeared.

4

If seams remain, repeat step 2 until they vanish. Turn the cupcake sideways and give it one firm shake to flick off any large water droplets. (Any remaining water will soon evaporate.)

Up Your Game

For a dipped swirl finish, hold the rounded tip of a small offset spatula at a 45-degree angle to the top of the iced cupcake, near the edge. Slowly rotating the turntable, drag the rounded tip through the icing to create a shallow spiral of icing into the center of the cupcake. At the center, lift the spatula with a flourish to create a sweet little peak of icing.

Peekaboo

Holy understatement, Batman. This design carries the graphic punch and dynamism of classic comic book illustrations. Good design doesn't have to be complicated. These cupcakes, with their iconic silhouettes, don't need speech balloons to communicate an enthusiastic KAPOW! After using the cookie cutter to punch out the middles of the sliced-off domes, be sure to save all the shapely cake cutouts. Sandwich two cutouts together with a little buttercream for darling sidekicks to accompany your cupcakes.

Cupcakes: 24 standard or mini cupcakes with domed tops, cooled

Pastry Bags: 1 bag

Tips: 1 extra-large round tip (or a coupler with no tip attached)

Buttercream: 5 cups (1.25 L)

Other Stuff: Small offset spatula
Small cookie cutter with a simple shape
Sugar crystals (clear or colored to match the icing)

Bag Prep: Fit the pastry bag with the round tip (or coupler) and fill it with about 2 cups (500 mL) icing. Refill as needed.

Cupcake Prep: Slice the domed tops off all the cupcakes. The more cake you have to work with when using the cookie cutter, the better for handling the delicate tops, so try to cut near the paper lining.

Decorating Steps

1 Hover and center the cookie cutter over a cupcake top. With even pressure, press the cutter down, removing the center portion of cake. Set the peekaboo tops aside. (Save the cutouts to make sandwich sidekicks, if desired.)

2 Working with one cupcake at a time, place each cupcake in the center of the turntable and ice it with a Button Top finish (page 223).

3 Coat the top of each iced cupcake by turning it upside down and dipping it in sugar crystals spread out on a small plate.

4 Gently cap each cupcake with a peekaboo cupcake top. Give the top a gentle press to secure it, making sure not to displace any of the icing.

Piece of Cake

Ditch the sugar crystals if you don't happen to have any on hand.

Up Your Game

These cupcakes look utterly smashing when you use vanilla cupcakes, a vibrant, deeply saturated icing color and jewel-toned sugar crystals.

Bits & Nibbles

- Cupcakes can pop out of the oven with plump domes or conveniently flat, depending on the recipe. For this project, you want domed cupcakes. In my experience, chocolate cake tends to dome more than vanilla.

- Filling a cupcake pan with extra batter will not help you make domed cupcakes. Too much batter usually leads to an unhappy overflow that adheres itself semipermanently to your cupcake pan. Maybe you already have a recipe that you know domes nicely, but if you don't, practice with a new recipe, such as the ones in chapter 2. Deflated results can hardly be considered a failure when the consequence is more cupcake consumption.

- Slicing off the top of a domed cupcake is just like slicing off the dome of a cake layer. Make sure you cut a large enough disk to accommodate the size of your cookie cutter. See page 36 for detailed instructions.

- I'm a sucker for happy rainbow-colored nonpareils, and you can easily swap them out with the sugar crystals. Ice your cupcakes in primary colors, use the rainbow nonpareils and use animal-shaped cookie cutters to create adorable animal-themed cupcakes.

Classic Soft-Serve Swirl

Exuberant and wonderfully whorled, the Classic Soft-Serve Swirl is the archetypical cupcake icing. So light and fluffy, it's the labradoodle puppy of the baking world: well-behaved, smart and irresistible. These cupcakes are fit for any company and ready at a moment's notice.

Cupcakes: 24 standard or mini cupcakes, cooled

Pastry Bags: 1 bag

Tips: 1 extra-large closed star tip, open star tip, French tip or round tip

Buttercream: 6 cups (1.5 L)

Bag Prep: Fit the pastry bag with the tip of your choice (see New Trick, page 232) and fill it with about 2 cups (500 mL) icing. Refill as needed.

Cupcake Prep: Place a cooled cupcake in the center of the turntable.

Up Your Game

Instead of decorating cupcakes one at a time, place 6 cupcakes in a widely spaced ring on the turntable. Decorating cupcakes in groups tends to make the job go more quickly.

New Trick: Cutting a Bag to Fit a Tip without a Coupler

Extra-large tips do not fit a standard coupler, and there are times when you will not want to use a coupler even when using a standard-size tip. Simply snip off the end of the pastry bag and drop the tip into the bag so that the narrow end pushes through the hole. Be forewarned that if the hole is too big, the tip will fall out when pressure is applied and the bag will be ruined. Start by snipping a small hole, then gradually increase the size of the hole until the tip fits snugly inside.

Decorating Steps

1 Hold the pastry bag vertically about ¼ to ⅓ inch (5 to 8 mm) above the cupcake, near the edge. Squeeze the bag with moderate pressure, anchoring the icing to the cupcake.

2 Continue to squeeze the bag while moving your arm in a small circular motion so that the icing coils around the cupcake.

3 As you finish the first rotation, overlap the starting point and then, without stopping, continue to pipe a smaller circle of icing on top of the first.

4 When the second circle is nearing completion, spiral in toward the center and make a small looping dollop on the top. A peak will naturally form as you decrease pressure and lift the bag.

Bits & Nibbles

- The nice thing about this swirled icing is that it works on either flat cupcakes or domed ones. No slicing required!

- If you're looking for a sleek, elegant cupcake, opt for a smooth round tip. If your mood leans toward fun and frisky, use a star tip to create deep ridges that are ideal for copious sprinkles.

- This technique will also work using a pastry bag fitted with a coupler and no tip.

- As you pipe the spiral, hold the decorating tip far enough away that the icing can drape gracefully into its natural tubular shape.

- If you prefer a shorter cupcake or one with less icing, hold the tip closer to the cupcake during the first circuit and closer to the first circle of icing during the second circuit, creating a more compact coil of icing.

- If you plan on traveling with your cupcakes, leave a small ring of cake un-iced around the edge of each cupcake. This will help prevent the cupcakes from becoming conjoined twins when packed snugly in a box.

Duet

When one color just isn't enough, use this technique to create a striking duet of contrasting colors. Instead of using a single pastry bag, this method separates the colors to keep them distinct and avoid comingled, muddy-hued mayhem.

Cupcakes: 24 standard or mini cupcakes, cooled

Pastry Bags: Two 12-inch (30 cm) bags
One 18-inch (45 cm) bag

Tips: 1 extra-large round tip

Buttercream: 3 cups (750 mL) each of two different colors

Other Stuff: Rubber band

Cupcake Prep: Place a cooled cupcake in the center of the turntable.

Bits & Nibbles

- Fill the bags with as much icing as you can manage at one time, because refilling them entails disassembling the conjoined small bags from the mother bag, so you don't want to do it more often than you need to.

- As you become confident in your icing technique, you can increase the size of the small bags to 16 inches (40 cm) and the mother bag to 24 inches (60 cm) to avoid needing to refill the bags multiple times.

Up Your Game

Two colors work great to support your favorite sports team, but you can use three colors to match a more colorful event or multiple hues to sweeten a groovy tie-dyed 70s-themed party. Simply add more small bags of icing to the large mother bag.

Decorating Steps

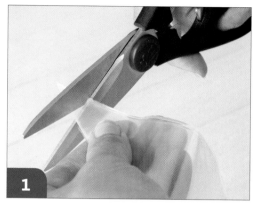

1 Cut the tips off the 12-inch (30 cm) bags, creating a hole in each about 1/3 inch (8 mm) in diameter.

2 Place one of the 12-inch (30 cm) bags in a mason jar or glass and fold down the edges over the sides of the jar, creating a wide opening. Fill the bag with 1 to 2 cups (250 to 500 mL) of one icing color.

3 Repeat step 2 with the second 12-inch (30 cm) bag and the other icing color.

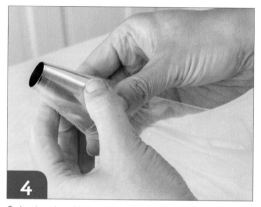

4 Snip the tip off the 18-inch (45 cm) bag so that the extra-large tip fits snugly inside (see New Trick, page 232).

5 Holding the bags of icing together, line up the tips and secure the tops of the bags by wrapping a rubber band around them, tying them together.

6 Drop the conjoined colored bags into the large mother bag, making sure that the cut tips nestle evenly within the large metal tip.

7

Flip the mother bag over and make sure that the two colors rest evenly within the metal tip and do not poke past the opening.

8

Give the bag a preparatory squeeze into a bowl to release air bubbles and combine the colors into a pleasing single coil of icing. Pipe the icing onto the cupcake as described in Classic Soft-Serve Swirl (page 231).

Rosette

The UK's Queen Elizabeth II, a peach of a gal and ever the garden enthusiast, boasts the honor of a rose christened in her name. The Queen Elizabeth II rose is a pink floribunda not so different from these cupcakes. With a flick of the wrist, you can create a garden of roses so sweet as to tickle Her Majesty, the royal gardeners and her cadre of corgis.

Cupcakes: 24 standard or mini cupcakes, cooled

Pastry Bags: 1 bag

Tips: 1 extra-large closed star tip

Buttercream: 6 cups (1.5 L)

Bag Prep: Cut the pastry bag to fit the star tip (see New Trick, page 232), drop in the tip and fill the bag with about 2 cups (500 mL) icing. Refill as needed.

Cupcake Prep: Place a cooled cupcake in the center of the turntable.

Bits & Nibbles

- The nice thing about rosette icing is that it works on either flat cupcakes or domed ones. No slicing required!

- The Classic Soft-Serve Swirl finish (page 231) starts near the edge of the cupcake and tapers up toward the center into a tall peak; conversely, the Rosette finish starts in the center and ends near the edge, with very little overlap and with the center as the lowest point.

- As you pipe the rosette, hold the decorating tip far enough away that the icing can drape gracefully into its natural tubular shape.

Decorating Steps

1 Hold the pastry bag vertically about ¼ to ⅓ inch (5 to 8 mm) above the center of the cupcake. Squeeze the bag with moderate pressure, anchoring the icing to the cupcake.

2 Continue to squeeze the bag, creating a small knot of icing around the anchor, then moving out toward the edge.

3 Keeping consistent pressure, begin a ring around the edges of the cupcake without overlapping the coils of icing.

4 As you near your starting point on the outer ring, decrease pressure and allow the icing to taper off as you connect with the starting point.

Up Your Game

Create an extraordinary rare breed of rose by striping the pastry bag with various hues of the same color. This will add depth, shadow and highlights to your icing rosettes. See page 50 for detailed instruction on striping bags.

Caterpillar Crawl

Flip your notions upside down, toss your assumptions aside and turn your cupcakes sideways. Think outside the cupcake box and create an undulating curve of caterpillar happiness.

Cupcakes: 12 standard cupcakes, baked in green liners, cooled

Pastry Bags: 1 bag without a coupler, 2 bags fitted with couplers

Tips: 1 extra-large round tip
Two #4 round tips

Buttercream: 4 cups (1 L) apple green
¼ cup (60 mL) black

Other Stuff: Small offset spatula
Extra-long presentation surface
24 green, 22 yellow, 1 pink and 2 blue banana-shaped hard candies
2 white candy-coated chocolate disks
Chocolate cake crumbs
Green sugar crystals or sprinkles

Bag Prep: Cut the pastry bag without a coupler to fit the extra-large round tip (see New Trick, page 232), drop in the tip and fill the bag with about 2 cups (500 mL) green icing. Fit the other pastry bags with the #4 round tips; fill one bag with 1 cup (250 mL) green icing and the other bag with the black icing.

Cupcake Prep: Using green icing from the bag with the extra-large round tip, ice all the cupcakes in the Classic Soft-Serve Swirl finish (page 231). Refill the bag as needed, and save a dollop of icing for step 5.

New Trick: Making Chocolate "Dirt"

Anytime you bake a chocolate cake or cupcakes, you can make chocolate cake crumbs to use as "dirt" in cake decorating projects. Make use of the sliced-off domed top of a cake layer or the one cupcake that is always smaller than the others. To make crumbs, wait until the cake has cooled completely, then pulse it in a food processor or rub the cake against a fine-mesh sieve until crumbled. Store cake crumbs in an airtight container in the freezer for up to 3 months.

Decorating Steps

1

For the face of the caterpillar, use the spatula to flatten the top and round the edges of one of the cupcakes, cleaning excess icing off the spatula as needed.

2

Map out the shape of the caterpillar by arranging all of the cupcakes, right side up, on the presentation surface, making two soft curves in the body. (Make sure to place the smooth cupcake at one end.)

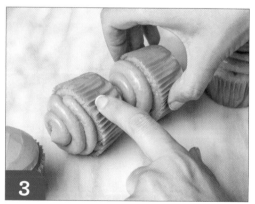

3

When you are satisfied with the caterpillar's shape, move the smooth cupcake away slightly and start to flip the swirled cupcakes on their sides, with the iced tops facing in the direction of the head.

4

As you flip the cupcakes, rest the peak of the icing on each cupcake against the bottom of the cupcake in front of it (without squashing the swirl).

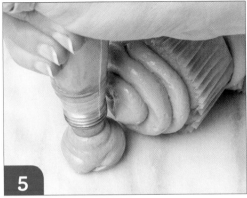

5

Using the remaining green icing from the bag with the extra-large tip, pipe a dollop of icing on the presentation surface, just in front of the first swirled cupcake.

6

Place the smooth cupcake at an angle on the dollop of icing so that the head of the caterpillar appears to be looking up at a jaunty angle.

7

Using green icing from the bag with the #4 round tip as glue, attach 2 green banana-shaped candies to each side of the first swirled cupcake as legs.

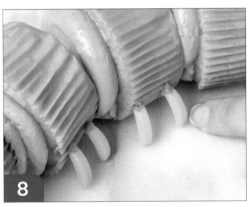

8

Alternating between pairs of yellow and green candies, continue to attach 4 legs to each of the remaining swirled cupcakes.

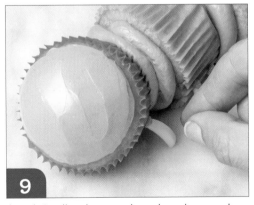

9

Attach 1 yellow banana-shaped candy on each side of the smooth cupcake.

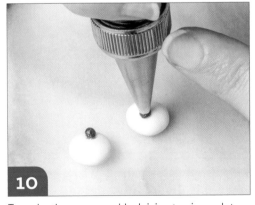

10

To make the eyes, use black icing to pipe a dot (see New Trick, page 146) onto each white candy-coated chocolate disk.

11

Place the eyes near the edge of the icing on either side of the smooth cupcake, about halfway down. Dip your finger in water and gently tap each black dot to flatten and smooth it.

12

Place the pink banana-shaped candy as a smile near the bottom of the smooth cupcake. Place the 2 blue banana candies as antennae at the top of the cupcake.

13

Add 3 to 4 clumps of chocolate cake crumbs on either side of the caterpillar, piled up around the feet to resemble clumps of dirt.

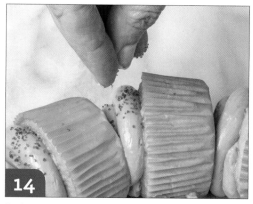

14

Sprinkle a light dusting of green sugar crystals on the icing segments of each swirled cupcake.

Bits & Nibbles

- After step 1, you can use the short end of a flexible plastic card to further refine the rounded face of the caterpillar. Slide the card around the sides and over the top of the cupcake. Make sure not to take off too much icing. My preferred tool is a New York City Metrocard, but you can use any plastic card that has some give and flex. I've seen people use medical insurance cards and gift cards. You can also make a card by cutting one out of a sour cream or cottage cheese lid. Make sure you cut with long, even strokes, because any jag or nick will show up on the surface of your icing.

Bits & Nibbles

- When making the caterpillar's eyes, where you pipe the pupils makes a difference in the direction the caterpillar is looking and his personality. You'll notice that in the photos of the completed project he's looking shyly to the side, but in the decorating step photos he is looking straight ahead. This is a great place to express your creativity. You can even play with piping different-sized pupils and see how it changes his character.

- I placed the blue antennae next to one another, arching out, but have fun and play with their placement to see how it changes the caterpillar's personality.

- Make this a fantastical rainbow-hued caterpillar by using multicolored cupcake liners and multiple icing colors, and alternate between all the colors for the candy legs.

Levity

If the mere act of eating cake doesn't send you over the moon, then maybe the lighthearted buoyancy of these cupcake balloons will do the trick.

Cupcakes: 16 standard cupcakes, baked in multicolored cupcake liners (optional), cooled and leveled

Pastry Bags: 9 disposable bags without couplers, 1 bag fitted with a coupler

Tips: #4 round tip

Buttercream: ⅔ cup (150 mL) each pale sky blue, royal blue, red, orange, purple, lavender, lime green, yellow and medium pink
⅓ cup (75 mL) white

Other Stuff: Nine 2- to 2½-inch (5 to 6 cm) round biscuit cutters with a lip (see Bits & Nibbles, page 252)
Small offset spatula
16 strands of thin poly ribbon in a variety of colors, each strand about 24 inches (60 cm) long
Scotch tape

Bag Prep: Cut each of the 9 disposable pastry bags to fit a biscuit cutter (see New Trick, page 232) and drop in a biscuit cutter. Fill each of the 9 bags with one of the first 9 icing colors. Fit the bag fitted with a coupler with the #4 round tip and fill it with white icing.

Cupcake Prep: Place a cooled cupcake in the center of the turntable.

Learn from My Mistakes

In retrospect, after sitting with this project and writing about it, I wish I had arranged the balloon strings to come down from multiple points at the bottom of the balloon bunch, and not just from one balloon on the bottom, to avoid the ribbon "tree trunk" look.

Piece of Cake

To simplify this project, you can cut down on the number of colors used.

New Trick: Highlights

Highlights are a series of lines and dots that are used to add dimension to objects. Where you place a highlight depends on how light would naturally strike the object. In Levity, the highlights represent light reflecting off the curved surface of balloons, so they run along the side of the balloons.

1. Fit a pastry bag with a round tip and fill it with icing in your highlight color. Start with the bag horizontal and lift it to a 60-degree angle, holding it ⅛ to ¼ inch (3 to 5 mm) above the surface you want to highlight.

2. Squeeze the bag with moderate pressure as you draw your hand in a curved line. As you near the end of the line, reduce pressure so that the tail of the highlight begins to taper. Continue to move your hand as you stop squeezing. This follow-through in hand motion will create a neat tapered tail.

3. Make 1 or 2 dots at the start and/or the end of the highlight line. Dots at the start of the line should be the same size or slightly thicker than the line; dots at the end of the line should be slightly thinner.

Decorating Steps

Before beginning to ice each cupcake, hold a pastry bag fitted with a biscuit cutter over a bowl, pointing slightly up. Squeeze lightly until a small amount of icing extrudes.

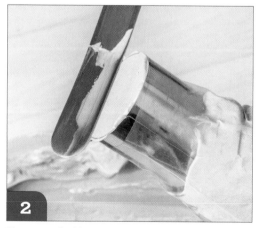

Use a small offset spatula to scrape the extruding icing into the bowl, leaving a smooth surface that is flush with the edge of the biscuit cutter.

3 Hold the bag with the biscuit cutter hovering ¼ to ½ inch (0.5 to 1 cm) above the cupcake. Squeeze with slow, even pressure so that the icing begins to puff out underneath the biscuit cutter.

4 While continuing to squeeze, draw your hand slowly up so that the icing makes a rounded dome. Stop squeezing before drawing your hand away.

5 Dip your finger in water and use it to gently tap down the peaked top and to smooth and round any edges. Repeat steps 1 to 5 with the remaining cupcakes, alternating among all the icing colors.

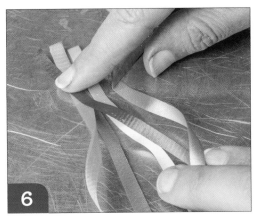

6 Gather the top ends of the ribbons together and secure them just below the center of your presentation surface with a piece of tape. Trail the ends over the side of the presentation surface.

7 Place 2 cupcakes on top of the ribbon ends. Continue to build the balloon bunch as desired to match your presentation surface, stacking the cupcakes in 2 layers and arranging the colors randomly.

8 Using white icing, add highlights (see New Trick, page 250) to the balloons on one side of the bunch, starting near the top of each cupcake and following the natural arc of the balloon.

Bits & Nibbles

- Before buying biscuit cutters, measure the diameter of the cups in your cupcake pan. You want to ensure that the diameter of the biscuit cutter is smaller than the diameter of the cupcake. Keep in mind that cupcakes shrink a bit and pull away from the side of the pan while baking.

- Admittedly, not everyone has 9 biscuit cutters of the same size, and if you don't plan on making balloon cupcakes often (or plan on going into the biscuit business), there are alternatives. Instead of piping the round biscuit cutter mounds, you can ice the cupcakes with a Button Top finish (see page 223). As long as you add highlights, they will still look like balloons. Another option is to ice the cupcakes in a Classic Soft-Serve Swirl finish (see page 231) and use a small offset spatula to flatten the top and round the edges. You can make an even smoother mound by refining the shape with a flexible plastic card (see Bits & Nibbles, page 246, for further details).

- Disposable pastry bags will stretch when you begin to pipe and the pressure builds. When cutting the bag for the biscuit cutter, cut the hole just big enough so that a small portion of the cutter will protrude.

- The shape of the balloon bunch will depend on the shape of your presentation surface. I made a bottom layer consisting of an outer ring of 9 cupcakes with 3 cupcakes nestled inside, and a top layer of 4 cupcakes balanced on the ones below. If your presentation surface is circular or square, make your balloon bunch round; if your presentation surface is oval or rectangular, make an oval bunch.

- Highlights can vary greatly depending on how light would naturally hit the surface of an object. To account for this variation, you can vary the number of dots added to the highlight line on each balloon. Dots above the piped line should be thicker than the line, while dots below it should be thinner and should get thinner still as they arc toward the bottom of the balloon.

Up Your Game

If you're feeling ambitious, add further whimsy to this project by creating some stand-alone cupcakes to feature alongside your balloon bouquet. Get creative with the theme, piping white puffy clouds on top of cupcakes iced in a sky blue Button Top finish (page 223) or decorating cupcakes with mini balloon bouquets made of multicolored candy-coated chocolate disks.

Index

Library and Archives Canada Cataloguing in Publication

Madden, Carey, 1974-, author
Buttercream basics : learn the art of buttercream decorating / Carey Madden.

Includes index.
ISBN 978-0-7788-0563-2 (softcover)

1. Cake decorating. 2. Icings (Confectionery). 3. Cookbooks. I. Title.

TX771.2.M338 2017   641.86'539   C2017-900071-3